CONSTITUTIONAL EQUILIBRIA

The Partisan Contingency of American Constitutional Law from the Jeffersonian "Revolution" to the Impeachment of Bill Clinton

John J. Janssen ¹⁰/₂₅/₈₁

University Press of America,® Inc.
Lanham · New York · Oxford

Copyright © 2000 by
University Press of America,® Inc.
4720 Boston Way
Lanham, Maryland 20706

12 Hid's Copse Rd.
Cumnor Hill, Oxford OX2 9JJ

Library of Congress Cataloging-in-Publication Data

Janssen, John J.
Constitutional equilibria : the partisan contingency of American
constitutional law from the Jeffersonian "revolution" to the
impeachment of Bill Clinton / John J. Janssen.
p.   cm
Includes bibliographical references.
1. Constitutional history—United States. 2. Constitutional law—
United States. 3. Law and politics. I. Title.
KF4541 .J353   2000   342.73'029—dc21   00-048016 CIP

ISBN 0-7618-1874-X (pbk. : alk. paper)
ISBN 0-7618-1873-1 (cloth : alk. paper)

⊖™ The paper used in this publication meets the minimum
requirements of American National Standard for Information
Sciences—Permanence of Paper for Printed Library Materials,
ANSI Z39.48—1984

CONTENTS

ACKNOWLEDGMENTS

This book is a derivation of the dissertation I researched and wrote at The University of Texas at Austin. Jim Fishkin supervised the dissertation and encouraged me to revise it for publication. I also owe special thanks to Yale law professor Bruce Ackerman, whose writings and support originally motivated this research project, and who generously agreed to serve as a member of my dissertation committee from the distance. I also have benefitted in countless ways from discussions of American constitutional development with my students at various colleges or universities and with colleagues in the legal profession. My wife, Jeanne Valentine, a scholar in her own right, encouraged me to develop the research here into a book, and has supported and endured this research from its early stages and through some tumultuous times. Thanks to all who have contributed to the book by way of critique, insight, and support, and, of course, all errors, whether of by act of omission or commission, are mine alone.

Chapter Two of the book derives from my article "Dualist Constitutional Theory and the Republican Revolution of 1800," 12 *Constitutional Commentary* 381 (Winter 1995). Excerpts unchanged have been used by permission.

INTRODUCTION

The argument of this book is simple. If we define the term "constitutional" to mean rules, procedures, or substantive laws fundamental to the republic by way of widespread political agreement or consensus, then what is considered constitutional by way of original text and formal amendment is not necessarily qualitatively superior to that which is considered constitutional merely by way of case law and institutional practices held in place by partisan balances of power. One analytical yardstick for assessing the legitimacy of latter constructs is whether the party or parties responsible for them have made sufficiently successful democratic overtures in the process of pursuing their policy agenda and in securing support for it.

In this book, I test this theory by way of examining the partisan policy agendas in place early in the history of the republic and examining how partisan realignments have shaped and re-shaped what has been amounted to constitutional policy. As many scholars have noted, this work bears some resemblance to the constitutional scholarship of Bruce Ackerman. Indeed, this research project reaches back to this author's days as a graduate student at Yale in Professor Ackerman's classroom. But, as best as I can tell, the enterprises are not quite the same. Bruce seeks to demonstrate how the legal problematics associated with ratification of the 1787 Constitution may be used an interpretive metaphor for addressing selected other problematic constitutional developments or transformations. To some extent I agree, but, more than anything, I mean only to ask whether a myriad of constitutional changes wrought by partisan realignments over the past couple of centuries can be squared with expectations for constitutional change at least implicit in Article V of the Constitution. I enjoy reading Professor Ackerman's thoughts on the matter, and hope he enjoys reading mine again.

CONSTITUTIONAL EQUILIBRIA

THE PARTISAN CONTINGENCY OF AMERICAN CONSTITUTIONAL LAW FROM THE JEFFERSONIAN "REVOLUTION" TO THE IMPEACHMENT OF BILL CLINTON

1. CONSTITUTIONAL EQUILIBRIA

I. The Basic Argument

The argument of this book is as follows: If we define the term "constitutional" to mean rules, procedures, or substantive laws fundamental to the republic by way of widespread political agreement or consensus, then what is considered constitutional by way of original text and formal amendment is not necessarily qualitatively superior to that which is considered constitutional merely by way of case law and institutional practices held in place by partisan balances of power. One analytical yardstick for assessing the legitimacy of latter constructs is whether the party or parties responsible for them have made sufficiently successful democratic overtures in the process of pursuing their policy agenda and in securing support for it.

What is perhaps less clear to the legal practitioner or other audiences is why one might~~spend~~considerable time developing the argument and making an attempt to apply the yardstick. Accordingly, some historical and interpretive context should precede the explanation of how the argument will be pursued in the subsequent chapters of the book.

II. Context

Constitutionalism in the United States refers to a concern with specifications for the allocation of powers to the national and state governments, and limitations on those powers as a means of protecting fundamental rights of American citizens at both levels. Articles I, II, and III of the United States Constitution, for example, specify the independent and shared functions of the legislative, executive, and judicial branches of the national government. Article IV stipulates that the citizens of each state shall be entitled to the privileges or immunities of citizens in the several states, and that each state shall give full faith and credit to public and judicial proceedings of every other state. Article V of the Constitution specifies the procedures for amendment of the Constitution, each of which requires extraordinary majoritarian consent. Hence American constitutions are understood to reflect and protect the widely-shared political values or preferences across both the national and state polities. Article VI, section 2 of the Constitution mandates that the Constitution, along with treaties and federal law, "shall be the supreme Law of the Land." Hence the United States Constitution may be understood to signify enforceable paradigmatic rules of national government, and changes to the Constitution are changes in such rules, not ordinary shifts in policy preferences or public opinion.

Despite the legalistic nature of the Constitution's provisions, however, the meaning of the Constitution has been transformed several times without the Article V amendment procedures having been respected. The First Amendment, to illustrate, expressly applies limits only the authority of the national government. The Amendment begins, "Congress shall make no law . . . ," and there is no question that the entire Bill of Rights originally was intended to limit the authority only of the national government. Even the U.S. Supreme Court acknowledged this in 1833.[1] No amendment expressly has changed the scope of the First Amendment, but federal courts today maintain that the First Amendment applies against state authority, too. The doctrinal justification for this application of the First Amendment to the states is judicial "incorporation" of many Bill of Rights provisions into the Fourteenth Amendment's express Due Process restrictions on state action.[2] However desirable it may be to enforce select Bill of Rights provisions against the states, however, the Fourteenth Amendment is textually vague as to its precise guarantees of individual liberty; and its legislative history suggests an intent far different from what has

---

[1] *Barron v. Baltimore*, 7 U.S. (Peters) 243 (1833).

[2] The first decision to announce the legitimate application of First Amendment restrictions on state government was *Gitlow v. New York*, 268 U.S. 652 (1925).

transpired under "incorporation."[3]

To further illustrate, in the early 1800s the Jeffersonians had made it a constitutional axiom that Congress lacked the authority to establish administrative programs not specified in the Constitution without first amending the constitution. The national bank thus was suspect and embattled even after *McCulloch v. Maryland*[4], wherein the Supreme Court had determined that Congress possessed the authority to charter the bank. In the 1930s, the Court had rejected some elements of Franklin Roosevelt's New Deal programs which proposed national government intervention in state and local affairs pursuant to the interstate commerce clause. Despite the expansions of federal commerce power over the course of the nineteenth century, there had remained until the mid-1930s, as a matter of constitutional doctrine, spheres of economic activity understood to be exclusively within state purview. But in 1937, apparently concerned about long-term institutional credibility amid a popular presidency which had threatened to manufacture a majoritarian voting bloc on it, the Court began to uphold New Deal legislation that it previously would have deemed unconstitutional; and in so doing, set the stage for an enormous expansion of national administrative authority over the course of the next several decades. The balance of power contemplated in the constitutional text ratified in 1789 ceased to exist in 1937, the constitutional order was transformed, and Article V never was invoked.

Such transformations in constitutional law have led to stern criticisms of contemporary American constitutional law. Judge Robert Bork, for example, who interprets the Constitution solely in relation to

---

[3]*See e.g.*, Raoul Berger, *Government By Judiciary: The Transformation of the Fourteenth Amendment* (Cambridge: Harvard University Press, 1977); Robert H. Bork, *The Tempting of America: The Political Seduction of the Law* (New York: Simon & Schuster, 1990); *see also* Mark Tushnet, *Red, White, and Blue: A Critical Analysis of Constitutional Law* (Cambridge: Harvard University Press, 1988). *But see* Akhil Reed Amar, "The Bill of Rights and the Fourteenth Amendment," 101 *Yale Law Journal* 1193 (1992), for an impressive alternative view.

[4]17 U.S. (4 Wheat.) 316 (1819).

the text and intent behind the provisions of the document, charges that the Constitution has been transformed without respect for Article V of the Constitution as a result of politically charged "nonorginalism" by lawyers and judges. As a result, he argues, "the integrity of the law already has been seriously undermined and the quality of its future remains very much in doubt."[5]

An avowed "critical" school of legal thought also has utilized both the plain language of American law and American history for purposes of demonstrating gaps between the constitutional text and its implications, inconsistencies in judicial rulings on constitutional questions, and the extent to which political considerations explain legal outcomes more than fidelity to neutral adjudicative principles.[6] In relation to American constitutional law, for example, Mark Tushnet concludes that

> the liberal tradition makes constitutional theory both necessary and impossible. It is necessary because it provides the restraints that the liberal tradition requires us to place on those in power, legislators and judges as well. It is impossible because no available approach to constitutional law can effectively restrain both legislators and judges: If we restrain the judges we leave legislators unconstrained; if we restrain the legislators we let the judges do what they want.[7]

In defense of contemporary constitutional terrain, William Harris has suggested that gaps between constitutional text and the prevailing constitutional order must be understood as implicitly characteristic of a constitutional order rooted in a text, given the interpretive process

---

[5]Robert H. Bork, *The Tempting of America: The Political Seduction of the Law*, (New York: Touchstone, 1990), p. 3.

[6]See the collection of critiques by a number of critical scholars in David Kairys ed., *The Politics of Law: A Progressive Critique*, rev. ed., (New York: Pantheon, 1990).

[7]Mark Tushnet, *Red, White, and Blue: A Critical Analysis of Constitutional Law*, (Cambridge: Harvard University Press, 1988), p. 313.

necessarily involved,[8] and this seems a very fair point. It also may be, as Gary Jacobsohn has argued, that constitutional aspirations do not have a specific blueprint for constitutional development and therefore leave considerable space for political application of these principles.[9] But one need not be an especially ardent originalist or critical scholar to recognize that the "incorporation" of Bill of Rights provisions and commerce clause developments mentioned above are instances of fundamental, not incremental constitutional change. These changes preclude the text of the Constitution from serving as an essentially reliable indicator–to legal professional and layman alike–of what constitutional law is today.

It is not the purpose of this book, nevertheless, to lament gaps between constitutional text and contemporary doctrine. Rather, its purpose is to demonstrate that a number of such gaps have occurred amid eras of partisan realignment in the United States, and that there have been patterns within these moments of transition which are analogous to the amendment processes contemplated in Article V of the Constitution. I attempt to offer some theoretical middle-ground between those who might disparage much of the contemporary constitutional order because of its infidelity to the original intent of the Constitution or its amendments and those who defend various informal constitutional amendments largely by disparaging the concept of "original intent." In mapping out this middle ground, I do not necessarily mean to endorse it or to disparage either more critical or more supportive views of the contemporary constitutional order. This book is written because the patterns are there, and the context gained by reviewing them is useful both to the legal practitioner and interested citizen. It is not meant as a strong endorsement of any particular method of hermeneutics. In my practice of law, I have found that the interpretations I give to any legal text before me are driven by an array of considerations which preclude such endorsement–save for the conviction that no interpretive question can be raised without beginning with the text.

---

[8]William F. Harris, *The Interpretable Constitution*, (Baltimore: Johns Hopkins University Press, 1993).

[9]Gary Jacobsohn, *The Supreme Court and the Decline of Constitutional Aspiration*, (Totowa: Rowman & Littlefield, 1986), p. 139.

To suggest that such patterns might be sufficient for imputing a legitimating integrity to the process of American constitutional development is at least to raise the possibility that American constitutionalism is fundamentally a political enterprise and less a legal one. The case for a political and not exclusively legal conception of "the constitutional" in the United States is two-fold. First, as Robert McCloskey observed, the Constitution of 1787 did not attempt to answer several major political questions of the day, especially the matter of the precise balance of power between the national and state governments, and an numerous junctures the meaning of the document was ambiguous.[10] Hence we should not be surprised by struggles between institutions, elites, or the electorate over the meaning of the Constitution. Partisanship in the United States, in fact, arose from disputes among the founding generation of elites as to the meaning of the Constitution. In his 1796 Farewell Address, for example, George Washington, warned against "the baneful effects of the spirit of party generally." Richard Hofstadter explains that in eighteenth-century American political theory, Americans "saw in parties only a distracting and divisive force representing the claims of unbridled, selfish, special interests."[11] The Framers thus appeared to recognize that parties would arise from time to time, but sought to create constitutional structures that would check and control parties.[12]

In the 1790s, nevertheless, as Federalists began implementing a commercialist and "strong central government" vision of the constitutional order that had just been established, fervent opposition to this agenda mounted, even from among those who had been architects of the new republic. Chief among the opponents to the Hamiltonian Federalists was Thomas Jefferson, who organized a rudimentary party to help oust Federalist John Adams from the Presidency in the 1800 election

---

[10]Robert G. McCloskey, *The American Supreme Court*, 2nd ed. (Chicago: University of Chicago Press, 1994), pp. 2-5.

[11]*See* Richard Hofstadter, *The Idea of a Party System: The Rise of Legitimate Opposition in the United States, 1780-1840*, (Berkeley: University of California Press, 1970). p. 40.

[12]*Ibid*, p. 53.

and implement his vision of the constitutional order. The Jeffersonian Republicans, which included James Madison, indeed had a more conservative vision of the Constitution, and, as author of the Declaration of Independence, Jefferson could speak with some authority as to guiding principles of the American revolution. Jefferson labeled his victory in 1800 a "second American revolution", and as the Jeffersonians entered office in 1801, they began to undo much of what the Federalists had done, and to reshape the constitutional terrain in their own image. During the Jeffersonian era, federal offices were greatly reduced, the federal Judiciary Act of 1801 was repealed, and federal common law indictments were declared invalid.[13] The Democratic-Republicans were the dominant party for the next two decades; the Federalist Party withered.

Second, while the Supreme Court may ostensibly serve as arbiter of the Constitution, its jurisprudence typically has gravitated toward support *for* prevailing political equilibria following the periodic re-orderings American political institutions and processes, even though the Court initially resists these re-orderings. Decades ago, Robert Dahl observed that the Supreme Court has tended to exercise its power of judicial review most often around "critical election" periods, *i.e.*, periods when an agitated electorate changes public policy, but it eventually falls in line with the new regime politics. [14] Studies of partisan realignments in the United States–in the 1830s, the 1850s, the 1890s, the 1930s, and perhaps the 1990s–make it all the more apparent that American political institutions have moved through stages of a relatively stable ordering, followed by disintegration, and then re-ordering. Each realigning period marks either the re-ordering or consolidation of constitutive institutions. If the Supreme Court eventually places its constitutional-arbiter imprimatur on the political order of the equilibrium, then constitutional doctrine would seem grounded in politics.

---

[13]It should be noted that James Madison, an important supporter of the Constitution and one of the principal authors of the *Federalist Papers* ultimately sided with the Jeffersonian persuasion by the early 1800s.

[14]*See* Robert A. Dahl, "Decision-Making in a Democracy: The Supreme Court as a National Policy-Maker," 6 *Journal of Public Law* 279-295 (1957).

Thus, because the term "constitutionalism," as a practical matter, reduces to what prove to be permanent institutions and practices amid the capacity of a democracy to change its political commitments, we may postulate that the public policies and practices which prove stable over relatively long periods of time reflect a sufficiently constitutive consensus, or "constitutional equilibrium." Because of the high degree of consensus required to formally amend the Constitution, many textual provisions likely would remain constant across various equilibria, but these also might tend to become the more politically trivial subjects of debt in comparison to issues of constitutional import less grounded in the text of the Constitution. But institutions and practices which are both of fundamental interest to the polity and divisive are likely to enjoy only modestly strong majoritarian support and relative permanence; and if they prove relatively permanent, they probably would be protected as matter of case law, not constitutional text. Even so, if what makes American constitutionalism legitimate is extraordinarily strong majoritarian support, the legitimacy of the transitions between constitutional equilibria depends on the nature of the transitions–specifically the extent to which they might be considered constitutively democratic.

III. A Test for the Legitimacy of Constitutional Equilibria

While the study of partisan realignments serves to elucidate the need for a political theory of American constitutionalism, realignments also present an opportunity for testing the nature of transitions between constitutional equilibria. By definition, that is, the transitions commenced by realignment politics are electorally driven and characterized by unusual electoral intensity. As defined by Walter Dean Burnham, realignments are massive shifts in party affiliation across the voting public caused by divisive political issues. "Realignments," he explains,

> arise from emergent tensions in society which, not adequately controlled by the organization or outputs of party politics as usual, escalate to a flash point; they are issue oriented phenomena, centrally, associated with these tensions and more or less leading to resolution adjustments; they result in significant transformations in the general shape of policy; and they have relatively profound after effects on the

roles played by institutional elites.[15]

If these processes have been, at least at times, sufficiently analogous to the processes for constitutional amendment provided in the text of the Constitution, a politically defensible theory of a constitutional equilibrium may be available where a legally defensible one is not.

Realignments scholarship suggests there have been five realignments in American history: Jefferson's rise to the presidency in 1800 and sustained Jeffersonian Republican leadership; the rise of the Democratic Party under the leadership of Jackson in the 1830s; the advent of the Republican Party in the 1854, sectionalism politics of the 1850s, and post-Civil War Republicanism; the Democratic challenge to the Republicans in the 1890s; and the successfully Democratic challenge to the Republicans in the 1930s and ensuing "New Deal" transformations.[16] The next five chapters of this book test the politics of five realignment periods in the United States for (a) challenges to the pre-existing constitutional equilibrium and (b) transitions analogous to the amendment provisions of the constitutional text.[17]

The test necessarily begins with the amendment provision of the Constitution. Article V of the Constitution reads, in part:

---

[15]Walter Dean Burnham, *Critical Elections and the Mainsprings of American Politics* (New York: W.W. Norton, 1970), p. 10.

[16]*See* Jerome M. Clubb, William H. Flanagan, and Nancy H. Zingale, *Partisan Realignment: Voters, Parties, and Government in American History* (Beverly Hills: Sage, 1980); James S. Sundquist, *Dynamics of the Party System: Alignment and Realignment of Political Parties in the United States*, rev. ed., (Washington: Brookings, 1983).

[17]In testing for integrity in the development of the constitutional order by analogy to the Article V amendment processes, this work bears a strong similarity to the work of Yale Law Professor Bruce Ackerman, most notably *We the People: Foundations* (Cambridge: Harvard University Press, 1991) and volume II of this work, *We the People: Transformations* (Cambridge: Harvard University Press, 1998). This probably should not be a surprise. See my discussion of this in the Introduction to this book.

> The Congress, whenever two thirds of both Houses shall deem it necessary, shall propose Amendments to this Constitution, or, on the Application of the Legislatures of two thirds of the several States shall call a Convention for proposing Amendments, which, in either Case, shall be valid to all Intents and Purposes, as Part of this Constitution, when ratified by the Legislatures of three fourths of the several States, or by Conventions in three fourths thereof, as the one or the other Mode of Ratification may be proposed by Congress ...[18]

These textual requirements of constitutional amendment may be abstracted into two basic conditions: (1) unusually strong popular consideration of proposed change to the Constitution, adjudged from a national perspective, and (2) exceptionally strong popular acquiescence toward the amendment initiative, again adjudged from a national perspective. Because the purpose of this book is essentially polemical, *i.e.*, it merely aims to show that a number of informal amendments can, post hoc, be democratically legitimated, the matter of whether these amendments procedures should be abstracted into such conditions is hereby consciously set aside.

The next step is to determine how each of these criteria may be tested for.

Unusually strong popular consideration of proposed change to the Constitution

This first condition may be satisfied by evidence of a highly mobilized electorate voting on constitutionally transformative proposals. By definition, realignments signify extraordinary electoral activity pertaining to fundamental policy issues. Yet it may help to inquire more precisely into whether the issues driving the electoral activity are constitutionally transformative, rather than just policy transformative. This may be ascertained by comparing the policy proposals–both actual and rhetorical–indicative of realignment politics with the dominant policies under the pre-existing partisan order. Some basic historical context and scholarly studies of American political development,

---

[18]U.S. Const., art. V.

including, of course, realignment scholarship, will be utilized to this end. An examination of judicial rulings also may be helpful (and may well be performed in realignment studies), because the exercise of judicial review, especially by the United States Supreme Court, can be understood to signal the inconsistency of some policy or practice with the prevailing understanding of fundamental law. Indeed, several scholars have observed that the Supreme Court tends to exercise its judicial review authority especially often during critical election periods.[19] Conceivably, however, the Court, like the other branches of the national government, could act, through judicial review, so as to attempt to move the polity toward a new constitutional equilibrium.[20]

Exceptionally strong popular acquiescence toward the amendment initiative

---

[19]*E.g.*, David Adamany,"Legitimacy, Realigning Elections and the Supreme Court," 3 *Wisconsin Law Review* 790 (1973); Richard Funston, "The Supreme Court and Critical Elections," 69 *American Political Science Review* 795 (1975); and John Gates, "The American Supreme Court and Electoral Realignment: A Critical Review," 8 *Social Science History* 267 (1984).

[20]It should be noted that while *Federalist* No. 63 speaks of the importance of deliberation for the republic and democratic decision-making, the Constitution aims to insure deliberation in the amendment process only by requiring extraordinary participation over the course of an arduous process. Article V says nothing about adequate information, reflective deliberation, or even fair political fights within the process of proposal or ratification, though these may be presupposed or expected to some degree. Therefore no attempt will or should be made to determine whether the American electorate, during realignments, either had sufficient information to make considered judgments or exercised their collective powers of deliberation particularly well. Hence this component of the test looks only for extraordinary participation regarding constitutionally transformative matters and ultimately, of course, evidence that the politics eventually stabilized in ways that demonstrably sustained or rejected particular transformative proposals. Even so, the political transformations of the Constitution to be examined here and the formal amendments to it since 1789 have served to move the American republic toward a more inclusive and participatory regime, with greater concern for fairness in matters of campaigns and elections.

For purposes of determining whether super-majorities win the struggles, either (1) widespread acceptance of the transformative policy or (2) an ultimate commitment to the status quo ante stand as the only possible criterion. Coordinate agreement across the three branches of the federal government, given the unique representative relationship each has to "the people themselves," as Bruce Ackerman observes,[21] probably most indicates a new, stable constitutional understanding. Whether transformations were approved will require consideration of the extent to which transformative policy proposals were implemented, embellished, compromised, or abandoned over time. The resulting partisan equilibrium, in other words, must be compared with the previous one. Little more will be needed than standard American history books, some basic historical statistics, and Supreme Court case law is virtually all that will be needed to learn of key legislative enactments, non-enactments and judicial rulings.

The final chapter of this book reviews the findings from the implementation of this test and suggests that the 1994 congressional elections marked the beginning of a prospective realignment, the politics of which manifested in an extraordinarily long government shutdown over budget politics and only the second impeachment of an American president in U.S. history.

---

[21]Bruce A. Ackerman, *We the People*, pp. 6-7. The idea of coordinate agreement among the three branches of government as dispositive indication of what is or is not constitutional is hardly new. This was the view during the Jeffersonian era. *See* Louis Fisher, *Constitutional Dialogues: Constitutional Interpretation as Political Process*, (Princeton: Princeton University Press, 1988).

2. THE JEFFERSONIAN "REVOLUTION"

Did the politics bringing Thomas Jefferson to the Presidency in 1800 and ousting the Federalists from power in the early 1800s result in both informal and legitimate constitutional change? As noted in the opening chapter, the textual requirements of the amendment process require, in essence, extraordinary consideration of proposed change to constitutional law and strongly popular acquiescence toward the proposed change. Each element of the amendment requirement, as also was noted, may be tested by particular criteria. With respect to the heightened deliberation requirement for this historical era, the policy conflict criterion leads to an examination of the controversy over the Alien and Sedition Acts and opposition to the government, anti-commercialism and civic virtue, and the federal judicial circuit. The mobilization of the electorate criterion focuses attention on studies of partisan realignment, with due attention to the fledgling nature of party machinery in 1800. The judicial behavior consideration implicates a review of *Marbury v. Madison*[1] and other cases in their political context. The application of these initial criteria lead to the conclusion that Jefferson's campaign constituted a moment of potentially transformative politics. Following Jefferson's election to the Presidency in 1800, the establishment of a legitimized party system, retrenchment of commercialism, a new naturalization act, and reform of the federal judiciary suggest that Jefferson's "revolution" generally was amenable to the electorate, suggesting that the second Article V requirement–namely popular acquiescence toward proposed changes–was met.[2]

---

[1]5 U.S. (1 Cranch) 137 (1803).

[2]But as Bruce Ackerman observes, Jefferson "did not trumpet his role as popular tribune very loudly." *See* Bruce Ackerman, *We the People: Foundations*, (Cambridge: Harvard University Press, 1991), p. 73.

WERE CONSTITUTIONALLY TRANSFORMATIVE POLICY PROPOSALS ASSOCIATED WITH THE 1800 PARTISAN REALIGNMENT

The Constitutional Status Quo Ante

Over the course of the 1790s, the Federalists and Republicans opposed each other on several fundamental issues: type of political economy, foreign policy and the nature of the American state, political organization and the public voice, and the legitimacy of organized opposition. For those readers not familiar with the major events of the 1790s up to 1800, however, the following summary might assist with the subsequent analysis of these issues.

To begin, the differences between the Federalists and Republicans were rooted in the division between the Federalists and Anti-Federalists. The former sought a larger central government more capable of securing commercial interests. The latter sought better government but a less powerful national government than the Federalists sought, and favored an agrarian political economy, largely because of its promise for securing civic virtue. Madison, Hamilton and Jefferson had been Federalists during the Constitutional Founding period, but Hamilton's economic program and the French Revolution would revive debates about political economy and central authority and divide some former allies into Federalist versus Republican camps.

In four reports to Congress, Hamilton, as Secretary of the Treasury, detailed his economic plans for the country. In short, he sought: revolutionary war debt consolidation by the central government, with securities issued to finance it; a national bank; duties and taxes as a means of making payments on the debt; and industrialization. Through groups and friends in the various states, Hamilton and the Federalists also sought more allegiance to the national government as a means of promoting their interests. They also favored a bigger standing army, fitting with the importance they attached to a strong national government. Opponents often viewed commercialism as suspect and also began to view the Federalists as nearly monarchical as the Crown had been.

As the French Revolution widened into the French-British war in the early 1790s, the Federalists and Republicans supported the side which better served their interests. According to Federalists, French principles of liberty, equality, and fraternity, which were supported by the Republicans, would destroy American society, if transplanted–a fear no doubt fed by the excesses of the Reign of Terror. When the Federalists, aiming to avoid renewed war with Britain, concluded the Jay Treaty in 1796, which granted Britain more favorable trade terms than the United States could offer any other nation, opponents charged that the Federalists were compromising the nation's security. French efforts to bribe American diplomats served as fodder for the Federalists. Near the close of the decade, a "quasi-war" at sea between the Americans and French had begun.

Republicans organized their opposition to Federalist programs by mobilizing the polity and press, with Jefferson becoming the ideological leader. Economic depression and the naval battles with France had served as the pretext for enactment by the Federalists of certain repressive measures, the most notable of which were the Alien and Sedition Acts. The Federalists purportedly designed the Acts as means for preserving national security. In the eyes of Republicans, however, the ulterior purpose of the Acts was to eliminate Republican opposition. The Republicans responded by drafting the Virginia and Kentucky Resolutions, which maintained that States could decide the constitutionality of federal legislation and interpose themselves between the citizenry and the central government.

President and Federalist John Adam's settlement of the "quasi-war" angered some Federalists, splitting the party's support; and in 1800, the Republicans won the Presidency and Vice-Presidency. Jefferson and fellow Republican Aaron Burr tied in the number of electoral votes garnered, so it fell to the House of Representatives to resolve the election. Jefferson was selected as president. The Federalists left office peaceably in 1801, but Adams staffed the federal judiciary with Federalist judges prior to his departure.

Constitutionally Transformative Proposals:

1. Commercialism is a threat to civic virtue

Throughout the 1790s, the Federalists sought to implement Hamilton's vision of commercialism by establishing a national bank, issuing securities on a centrally consolidated national debt, and levying taxes and duties for government-sponsored internal improvements.[3] In 1793, in direct response to Hamilton's program, Jefferson outlined a Republican agenda. It included abolition of the national bank, reduction of the impost tax, repeal of the excise tax, and exclusion of public debt-holders from Congress.[4] Over the course of the decade, Jefferson would emerge as the political leader of the Republican party.[5] Activist contributors to newspapers and political pamphleteers would also develop the Republican agenda and communicate it to the public, often citing the

---

[3]Conflict over Alexander Hamilton's economic vision for the country antedated the ratification of the Constitution. Thus the same basic economic program that Hamilton advanced in 1790 and 1791, as Joseph Charles suggests, would hardly seem adequate cause for the ensuing strife between Federalists and Republicans. *See* Joseph Charles, *The Origins of the American Party System* (Institute of Early American History and Culture, 1956), p. 97. The resulting acrimony may be best explained by what Lance Banning describes as the suffused hypersensitivity to State encroachment on liberty, informed by Revolutionary maxims. *See* Lance Banning, *The Jeffersonian Persuasion* (Ithaca: Cornell University Press, 1978), p. 127.

[4]Lance Banning, *The Jeffersonian Persuasion, id.*, p. 181.

[5]Jefferson's predilection for agrarian interests had been public knowledge since his *Notes on the State of Virginia*, where he commented that "those who labor in the earth are the chosen people of God." *See* Noble E. Cunningham, Jr., *The Jeffersonian Republicans* (Chapel Hill: University of North Carolina Press, 1957), pp. 220-21. (The comment may be found in Thomas Jefferson, *Notes on the State of Virginia* (W. Peden ed., New York: W.W. Norton, 1954), pp. 164-65. When Jefferson's criticism of Hamilton's economic program was printed without his knowledge or approval, a Federalist propaganda campaign followed. A series of political essays penned by "Publicola," who was actually John Quincy Adams, defended Federalist policies. Federalists positions were also advanced in *Discourses on Davila*. Madison and Jefferson responded to the campaign by helping to establish a national newspaper that would print articles opposing printed Federalist positions--the *National Gazette*. Between 1791 and 1793, the *Gazette* would serve as a forum for developing a cohesive Republican party ideology. *See* Lance Banning, *supra* note 3 at 155-60, 182-94; *see also* Noble E. Cunningham, Jr., *The Jeffersonian Republicans*, *supra*, at 10-15.

dangers to the farmer and civic virtue that commercialism posed.[6] The 1800 Republican party platform, reproduced below as printed in the Philadelphia *Aurora*, would promise voters: decrease of public debt, reduced taxes, no loans, no excises, reduced public salaries, and a system of economy and care of the public money.[7]

2. *The Republic Must Not Be Aristocratic in Nature*

The French Revolution would force American leaders, as Richard Hofstadter explains, "to make decisions about foreign policy that were bound to have either a British or a French bias, that made the party breach unnegotiable and almost irreconcilable."[8] Jay's treaty with Britain in 1794, amid the war between Britain and France, would foment the division. Prior to the treaty, the British had announced plans to remain in Northwest territory indefinitely and also seized cargoes of American ships carrying provisions to or from certain French islands. Jay's treaty

---

[6]Political pamphlets were also a means of Republican political expression. Through the medium, George Logan, who had contributed to the *Gazette* under the pen name "An American Farmer," attacked programs that threatened to depress the agricultural population and attributed the economic woes of the country to those citizens "infatuated with the false principles of the government of Great Britain." *See* Banning, *supra*, note 3 at pp. 186-92. This association of the Federalists with Britain would become more important, indeed politically divisive, later in the decade. The most important pamphleteer of the decade was John Taylor, whose *An Enquiry into Principles and Tendency of Certain Public Measures* (1794) stood nearly as an unofficial statement of Republican principles. Taylor saw Federalist programs as premised on a misinterpretation of the Constitution and favored strict construction of the text. He also maintained that since government depends on the people for its life, it must always seek the general good. The National Bank, then, had to be dismantled, as it served to make the rich richer and the poor poorer. *See* Banning, pp. 192-200.

[7]Cunningham, *The Jeffersonian Republicans*, supra n. 5, p. 214 (reproducing the party ticket printed in the Philadelphia *Aurora*, October 14, 1800).

[8]Richard Hofstadter, *The Idea of a Party System: The Rise of Legitimate Opposition in the United States, 1780-1840*, (Berkeley: University of California Press, 1969), p. 88.

stipulated that Britain would leave its Northwest posts, expand commerce with American states, and pursue an arbitrated settlement of prewar debts and other disputes. The Americans agreed not to trade with colonies of the enemies of Britain, to grant Britain most-favored-nation trading status, and that many American debts to British merchants would be paid by the American government.[9]

The Federalists maintained the Jay treaty was essential for national security. It would reduce tensions with Britain, a military power capable of inflicting substantial damages on the American states. In so doing, the treaty also would preserve the progress of Hamilton's economic programs and thereby strengthen the new republic. Rejecting the treaty, they charged, would force the American states into an alliance with France and that country's global struggles.[10] An alliance with France would engender increased support among the states for the social-leveling and subsequent dangers to the American state inherent in too much "liberty, equality, and fraternity.[11] As for whether the treaty limitations imposed on Congress regarding the regulation of commerce violated the Constitution, Federalists simply maintained that the Constitution assigned the president authority to make treaties with the Senate's advice and consent.[12]

Republicans loathed the treaty. It compromised national interests by renouncing "sequestration, nonintercourse, and discrimination" against

---

[9]Richard Buel comments on the risks the United States took in relinquishing the possibility of sequestration, given the U.S.Britain trade imbalance: "Everyone knew that, given the balance of trade between the two nations, British debts in America would always far exceed American debts in Britain. Thus by giving up an instrument of substantial power over Britain while Britain gave up nothing, the United States risked permanent subordination." Richard Buel, Jr., *Securing the Revolution* (Ithaca: Cornell University Press, 1972), p. 63.

[10]*Id.* at 69.

[11]See the discussion of the Jay treaty in John Garraty and Peter Gay eds., *The Columbia History of the World* (New York: Harper & Row, 1972), p. 795.

[12]Buel, *Securing the Revolution*, p. 70.

Britain--"the only weapons [the United States] possessed for bringing Great Britain to terms short of war."[13] The treaty, Republicans charged, clearly aligned the United States with Britain against France, the greater defender of liberty. With regard to the presidential authority to negotiate the treaty, Republicans maintained that Jay's treaty represented an unconstitutional aggrandizement of executive authority: it ultimately could lodge all congressional and judicial power in the hands of the president and Senate. As Richard Buel comments, Republicans saw the exercise of presidential power represented in Jay's treaty as "an argument for aristocracy and monarchy."[14] In 1799, Jefferson noted his opposition to "monarchising" features of the Constitution.[15]

3. Political Organization Is a Legitimate Means for Expressing Public Opinion

The framers of the Constitution generally denounced political parties as divisive forces that would threaten the fabric of the republic. Richard Hofstadter observes that "the idea of a legitimate opposition–recognized opposition, organized, and free enough in its activities to be able to displace an existing government by peaceful means–is an immensely sophisticated idea" that the Framers of the Constitution had neither developed nor imagined at the republic's inception.[16] But party organization began with the rise of opposition to Hamilton's economic program announced in 1790, whereupon Federalists responded by building coalitions of support. Over time, party organization would move from Congress to state machinery, and as party conflict evolved, Cunningham observes, "warnings against the dangers and evils of parties

---

[13]*Id.* at 63.

[14]Id. at 70.

[15]Cunningham, *supra*, n. 5, p. 211 (quoting Jefferson to Elbridge Gerry, January 26, 1799, *The Writings of Thomas Jefferson* (Ford ed. 1892-99) Vol. VII, pp. 327-29.

[16]Hofstadter, *The Idea of a Party System*, p. 8.

grew louder and were heard more often."[17]

Both Republicans and Federalists acknowledged the political vices usually associated with parties, so that neither tended to view their party machinery as an addendum to the American political process. Republicans understood their party machinery as essential to preserving the Union; once the crisis ended, the machinery would dissolve. The Federalists were more vociferous in denouncing political parties, urging instead common support of the government.[18] But they nurtured their party organizations so as to compete with Republican political forces. By 1796, candidates for public office were running on party tickets, and some states were using party organizations to nominate candidates. By 1800, party committees at the local level had become means of informing and mobilizing voters.

As the 1800 election approached, the Republicans would implement an unprecedented programmatic effort to mobilize the public through party machinery and elevate the significance of national elections for the presidency. They sought not only to improve their party machinery across all states, but also to reform laws regarding the choice of presidential electors, so as to favor Republicans.[19] Initially, Federalists denounced partisan attempts to control the selection of presidential electors, but ultimately they too would encourage biased reform in elector selection laws.[20]

4. Criticism of the Government Is Legitimate

Following the French seizures of American ships in response to the Jay

---

[17]Cunningham, *The Jeffersonian Republicans*, p. 140

[18]*Id.*, p. 141 (noting that many sermons in New England addressed the evils of parties and that the "political parsons" delivering the sermons often had Republicans in mind.)

[19]*Id.*, pp. 144-47.

[20]*Id.*

Treaty, the Federalists secured passage of the Alien and Sedition Acts.[21] The Alien Act authorized the president to expel, imprison or fine dangerous aliens, contingent upon declaration of war. The Sedition Act criminalized any organization, conspiracy or open criticism of the government or any of its agents, and could apply to domestic political opposition in times of peace.

The Federalists maintained that the Acts were essential for national security. John Marshall, one of the most eloquent Federalist spokesmen, defended the Acts in a 1798 address. Under the Constitution, he observed, Congress has the authority to define and punish offenses against the law of nations, and "it is an offence [sic] against that law [of nations] to become dangerous to the peace and safety or to be concerned in any treasonable or secret machinations against the government of the country in which he resides."[22] Marshall interpreted both Congress' power to suppress rebellions and the guarantee to each state of a republican form of government under the Constitution to imply an affirmative duty on the central government to protect states from invasion, with congressional access to any necessary means for executing the duty. Removing dangerous aliens, he maintained, is a legitimate

---

[21]A brief history of the Acts might help. The French had responded to the Jay Treaty by seizing American ships, just as the British had done prior to the Treaty. Diplomatic efforts failed to resolve the conflicts and led to limited hostilities between French and American forces. The Republicans were outraged at the hostilities, but their call for a review of the failed diplomatic proceedings led to revelation of the embarrassing XYZ affair, in which French diplomats requested a loan, a bribe and an apology (for remarks made by Adams) from U.S. diplomats. The Republicans maintained that the disclosure was yet another attempt by the Federalists to malign France and destroy support for the principles of liberty enshrined by the French republic. But the hostilities transpiring and the XYZ affair led public opinion to turn against France. The Federalists then began a limited naval war with the French, which would last two years. And during the patriotic fervor of this moment, the Federalists managed to enact the Alien and Sedition Acts.

[22]J. Marshall, Address on Constitutionality of Alien and Sedition Laws, in M. Frisch and R. Stevens eds., *The Political Thought of American Statesmen* (Itasca: F.E. Peacock, 1973), p. 106.

action for such protection of the states.[23] The principle could be abused, "but the possibility of abusing a principle is never supposed to be a correct argument against its use."[24] The attacks on the sedition law, moreover, were unwarranted, because to deny government the power to punish "false, scandalous and malicious" writings "would be to assert the inability of our nation to preserve its own peace, and to protect themselves from the attempt of wicked citizens . . . incessantly employed in devising means to disturb the public peace." The Constitution forbids all abridgement of the freedom of the press, but it is nevertheless necessary to inquire whether an act in question "does in fact *abridge* the freedom of the press . . . A punishment of . . . licentiousness is not considered as a restriction of the freedom of the press."[25]

The Republicans argued that the Acts, particularly the sedition law, were oppressive, unconstitutional measures, inconsistent with fundamental liberties of criminal procedure and free expression guaranteed under the Constitution. Under the sedition law, a person might be convicted by a jury for merely having an opinion, unless he could persuade the jury his opinion was true. The sedition law would not only intimidate critics of the government and those who would print criticisms, but, as Madison charges, make elections meaningless. The law would insulate incumbents from opponents' criticisms, so that voters "will be compelled to make their election between competitors whose pretensions they are not permitted by the act equally to examine, to discuss and to ascertain."[26]

Jefferson and Madison, respectively, wrote the Republican opposition ideology into the resolutions issued by the Kentucky and Virginia legislatures in response to the Alien and Sedition Acts. Madison

---

[23] *Id.*, p. 107.

[24] *Id.*, p. 108.

[25] *Id.*, p. 113.

[26] Buel, *Securing the Revolution*, p. 250 (quoting James Madison's "Report of the Committee," from *The Writings of James Madison*, Vol. VI (G. Hunt ed. 1900-1910), pp. 397-98.

advanced the doctrine of interposition–that the states could judge the constitutionality of federal acts and interpose themselves between their citizens and illegitimate actions by the central government. He admonished that liberal construction of the Constitution would serve to increase centralized authority, thereby increasing the tendency toward monarchy. He also maintained that the sedition law abridged the First Amendment guarantee of free expression of ideas, the very principle essential to the survival of free society.[27] Jefferson emphasized the authority reserved to the States and the people themselves under the Constitution. "[E]very State has a natural right in cases not within the compact, . . . to nullify of their own authority all assumptions of power by others within their limits: that without this right, they would be under the dominion, absolute and unlimited, of whosoever might exercise this right of judgment for them."[28]

5. Expansive Federal Court Power

The Federalists staffed the first Supreme Court with Federalists, and early Court decisions reflected partisan leanings and gave rise to livid Republican criticism. In the 1796 case *Ware v. Hylton*[29], the Court declared invalid a Virginia statute sequestering pre-Revolutionary War debts of British creditors. The peace treaty between the Americans and British stipulated no impediments on the recovery by British subjects of debts due them by Americans. The Court held that the treaty nullified earlier Virginia law, destroyed payments made under it, revived the debt, and gave rights of recovery against the debtor, notwithstanding payment made under the authority of state law. The Court's subordination of state law to treaties with respect to the very sensitive issue of Revolutionary debts "led to Republican criticism of the judges as Pro-British

---

[27]Daniel Sisson, *The American Revolution of 1800*, (New York: Alfred A. Knopf, 1974), p. 336.

[28]Thomas Jefferson, Draft of the Kentucky Resolutions, in M. Frisch and R. Stevens eds., *The Political Thought of American Statesmen*, p. 17.

[29]3 U.S. (3 Dall.) 199 (1796).

Federalists."[30]

Chisholm v. Georgia[31], decided in 1793, involved the question whether the federal judiciary may summon a state as defendant and adjudicate its rights or liabilities. Despite assurances in *The Federalist Papers* that such jurisdiction would be unavailable to federal courts, the Supreme Court held that federal courts do possess such authority. The decision resulted in a Republican-led "states' rights" backlash and the Republicans proposed the Eleventh Amendment, which would preclude federal jurisdiction in cases of suits against states. The Federalists ultimately conceded the Eleventh Amendment in 1798, amid "the rising Republican clamor . . . for a new constitutional convention . . . ."[32] The Eleventh Amendment notwithstanding, *Chisholm* did represent the Federalist vision of consolidating power under a central government.

The common law also became a divisive political issue in the 1790s. In short, the question was whether federal common law jurisdiction existed. The issue had been raised in *United States v. Worrall*[33], where the losing defense attorney, a Republican, had maintained that the criminal common law charge against his client contravened the limitations on federal power represented in the Tenth Amendment. But during the foreign policy crisis of 1798, the Federalists sought to prosecute seditious libel in federal courts under the common law, and their success led to passage of the Judiciary Act of 1801, which extended the jurisdiction of federal courts to all cases in law and equity arising under the U.S. Constitution and federal law.

The Sedition Act would soon provide the statutory basis for sedition

---

[30]Alfred Kelly, Winfred A. Harbison, and Herman Belz, *The American Constitution: Its Origins and Development*, 6th ed. (New York: W.W. Norton, 1983), p. 166.

[31]2 U.S. (2 Dall.) 419 (1793).

[32]*See* Calvin R. Massey, "State Sovereignty and the Tenth and Eleventh Amendments," 56 *University of Chicago Law Review* 113 (1989).

[33]2 U.S. (2 Dall.) 384 (1798).

prosecution, but until then, the sweeping jurisdiction granted the federal courts under the Judiciary Act alerted Republicans to the possibility that a national common law might be presumed by the Federalists. Common law reached virtually every area of life, so to assume a national common law, Republicans charged, would mean granting to Congress general legislative power, a violation of the limited national power guaranteed by the Constitution. In 1800 Jefferson commented:

> If the principle were to prevail of a common law being in force in the U.S., [it would] possess the general government at once of all the powers of the state governments and reduce [the country] to a single consolidated government.[34]

DID ANY CONSTITUTIONALLY TRANSFORMATIVE PROPOSALS HAVE WIDESPREAD SUPPORT BEYOND THE REALIGNING ERA?

The partisan equilibrium following the 1800 displacement favored the Republicans. The inquiry now turns to whether widespread acceptance of Republican ideology and programs may be said to have followed the party's rise to power. "Widespread acceptance" is operationalized by looking to the long-term status of policies and principles advanced by the Republicans and any indicators that the transformative policies and principles gained, for at least a stable historical moment, strong public support.

1. Retrenchment of Commercialism

Once President, Jefferson quickly sought to retrench the economic program on which the Federalists had embarked. In the first session of Congress after his election, Jefferson considered abolishing the whole system of internal taxation the Federalists had adopted. Fearing the effects of such a sudden cutoff in revenues, the plan implemented was not so ambitious, but enough so that governmental cutbacks were required. Indeed, upon retrenchment, one half of federal administrative offices

---

[34]Kelly, Harbison, and Belz, *The American Constitution: Its Origins and Development*, p. 171 (quoting Jefferson, no cite provided).

were abolished, with many cutbacks in the military.[35]

Retrenchment, however, was not complete. The Republicans spared the national bank–the institution incommensurable with the Republican vision of political economy. Jefferson maintained that since it had already been established, he could not in good faith abolish it.[36] Madison, in fact, came to support the bank. The War of 1812 required the development of manufactures and war material, and this would further distort the agrarian vision of political economy.[37] The Louisiana Purchase would greatly raise the public debt, but it had fallen before and would eventually fall again–dramatically so.[38] Following the 1812 war, sectional differences over matters of economic development, such as tariffs and internal improvements, would fundamentally divide Republicans and serve to erode their "common good" ideology.[39] Those partisans carrying the Republican banners of 1798 and 1800 became known as the "old Republicans." "New Republicans," Leonard White explains, included a former staunch Federalist, John Quincy Adams, and were "nationalist in outlook . . . ." White continues:

> They stood for the broad construction of national power, for an active employment of those powers, for a strong navy, for a well-organized army, for a United States Bank, for a tariff, for internal improvements, and a foreign policy that looked toward the further acquisition of territory."[40]

These new Republicans were a policy force, but, as Richard Ellis notes,

---

[35]*Id.*, p. 23.

[36]Russell L. Hanson, *The Democratic Imagination in America: Conversations with Our Past* (Princeton: Princeton University Press, 1985), pp. 103-04.

[37]*Id.*, p. 105.

[38]Banning, *The Jeffersonian Persuasion*, p. 279.

[39]Hanson, *The Democratic Imagination*, p. 106.

[40]Leonard D. White, *The Jeffersonians* (New York: MacMillan, 1951), p. 14.

they were less successful in establishing a federal program of improvements than old Republicans, many of whom had voted to re-establish the bank on the belief that it was the only means of securing economic stability following the 1812 war and proliferation of banks.[41] Even so, in 1828 the new-Republican Secretary of Treasury cited Alexander Hamilton as an authority on economic policy.[42]

2. Legitimate Opposition Sustained

Given the popular and intellectual disdain for political parties, both the Republicans and Federalists had conceived their party machinery as aberrations necessary for the preservation of the Union. But party organizations endured beyond the rise of the Republicans in 1800. Shortly after the election, in fact, the party system would make institutional changes in American politics. First, it marked the triumph of parties over politicians. Before the advent of parties, candidates in elections were judged according to character, personality, qualifications or integrity. With party affiliation becoming a more relevant consideration, the stigma attached to campaigning for office declined; the effort could be viewed as a contribution to the party cause. Indeed, by 1800, as Cunningham observes, it was a political asset to have the reputation of being a party man.[43] Party affiliation revealed to voters a candidate's policy preferences and perhaps even his moral character, both of which were important electoral considerations. In the next two decades, civic virtue–a primary tenet of Republicanism–became identified with party regularity.[44]

Second, as James Ceasar observes, enduring party machinery led to a

---

[41]Richard E. Ellis, "The Persistence of Antifederalism after 1789," in R. Beeman et al. eds., *Beyond Confederation* (Chapel Hill: University of North Carolina Press, 1987).

[42]*Id.*, p. 14.

[43]Cunningham, *The Jeffersonian Republicans*, p. 254.

[44]*Id.*, pp. 254-55; *see also* Russell L. Hanson, *The Democratic Imagination*, pp. 118-19.

transformation of the presidential selection system. Republicans introduced and, by their actions, "helped to legitimize the idea of the candidate as party leader."[45] They also demonstrated that victory in national elections could supply energy for the president's agenda. And they implemented changes in electoral institutions, including the congressional caucus for purposes of candidate nominations and the Twelfth Amendment, which allowed the separation of electoral votes for president and vice-president.[46]

Also, it is important to note that the foreign born, who were direct targets of the Alien and Sedition laws, faced a different governmental posture following the Republican victory. First, the Alien and Sedition laws had expired and were not renewed. Second, the Republicans, in the first session of Congress after the election, passed a new naturalization act, restoring the requirements under Washington's administration. "Five years' residence would once more suffice to make the foreign-born an American citizen, with three years' notice of intention."[47]

3. Weakened Central Government

In an American history text, Gordon Wood observes that during the first three decades of the 1800s, particularly after Jefferson left the presidency, "the United States was weaker than at any other time in its national history."[48] "The early government," he observes, "was ... small almost beyond imagination."[49] Jefferson sought to weaken the central

---

[45]James W. Ceasar, *Presidential Selection: Theory and Development* (Princeton: Princeton University Press, 1979), p. 96.

[46]*Id.*

[47]James Schouler, *History of the United States of American Under the Constitution*, Vol. II, rev. ed., (Dodd, Mead, & Co., 1970), p. 27.

[48]Bernard Bailyn et al., *The Great Republic: A History of the American People*, 2nd ed., Vol. 1 (Lexington: D.C. Heath & Co., 1981), p. 280 (Wood is the author of a particular section of the book).

[49]*Id.*, p. 28.

government by retrenching the Hamiltonian economic program, dismantling the Federalist's federal judicial circuitry program and encouraging strict construction of the Constitution. Economic retrenchment, as explained above, was partially achieved. Jefferson did execute the Louisiana Purchase, which may be understood as an illustration of the enormous power the national government retained. But Ellis notes that the turnover of two-thirds of the House of Representatives in the 1816 election "put a halt to any further nationalist legislation."[50] In his classic review of the Jeffersonian era, James Sterling Young explains that the slight function of the national government--a central premise of Jeffersonian orthodoxy–explained its small size, citizen ambivalence toward it, and the initial failure of the Washington, D.C. capital as a planned, self-financing community.[51]

With regard to the federal judiciary in particular, the Republicans repealed the 1801 Judiciary Act, which had given expansive jurisdiction to federal courts. The Judiciary Act of 1789 was thus revived, and the Republicans passed another law providing for annual instead of semi-annual sessions of the Supreme Court.

If the Supreme Court is a barometer of higher law, then Republican success in the retrenchment of national governmental power may be gleaned from John Marshall's opinion in *Marbury v. Madison*. Prior to the 1803 decision, the Federalists had attempted three times to challenge the constitutionality of the Republican-led repeal of the 1801 Judiciary Act (which had resulted in Federalist judges favoring governmental prosecutions under the Alien and Sedition Acts), but each effort failed. There is little doubt that Marshall's defense of judicial review in the Supreme Court reflects Federalist interests, but his refusal to issue the mandamus suggests he recognized the possibility that such an order would be ignored. As James O'Fallon comments, "*Marbury* was born out

---

[50]See Ellis, *supra* n 41, p. 307.

[51]James Sterling Young, *The Washington Community, 1800-1828*, (New York: Harcourt, Brace, Jovanovich, 1966), pp. 13-37.

of political defeat."[52]   It is also interesting to note that in 1804 the Republicans would seek to impeach one of the most partisan Federalist judges, Samuel Chase, who arguably influenced Marshall's analysis in *Marbury* of the Supreme Court's jurisdiction.[53]   Impeachment would remove John Pickering from the federal bench, not Chase–a bitter disappointment for Jefferson.[54]

The federal common law question would also eventually be resolved in favor of the Republicans. In *United States v. Hudson and Goodwin*[55], the Supreme Court held that federal common law indictments (which here had been issued at the bequest of Republicans) were invalid because federal courts had no common law jurisdiction.   The Court maintained

---

[52]James O'Fallon, "Marbury," 44 *Stanford Law Review* 219 (1992), p. 259. Kelly, Harbison and Belz take a similar position:

> Though critical of the executive, Marshall refused to issue the mandamus, thus letting the administration win the battle.   He recognized, moreover, a sphere of discretionary political action in which the judiciary lacked competence to judge of constitutionality or determine the meaning of the Constitution. Acquiescing to this extent in the political power that Jefferson represented, Marshall nevertheless established a limit beyond which the political branches could not go.... Bold as Marshall's strategy was ..., his assertion of judicial review was thus basically defensive.

Kelly, Harbison, and Belz, *The American Constitution*, p. 181.

[53]O'Fallon, *supra*, n. 53, pp. 253-54.

[54]According to George Brown Tindall, Jefferson viewed the impeachment process as a "farce" after Chase's acquittal.   Tindall, *America, A Narrative History*, Vol. I (New York: W.W. Norton, 1984), p. 326. (Tindall provides no cite for Jefferson's comment.)

[55]11 U.S. (7 Cranch) 32 (1812).

a strict construction view of constitutional interpretation.[56] Ironically, the charge can be made that Jefferson abandoned his strict construction principle in effecting the Louisiana Purchase.[57] Also, it is important to recognize that the majority opinion in *Fletcher v. Peck*[58], penned by Marshall, advances an interpretation of the Constitution's contract clause that can, as it did in this case, limit state power: "When . . . a law is in its nature a contract, when absolute rights have vested under that contract, a [legislative] repeal of the law cannot divest those rights."[59] Under Marshall and Justice Story, moreover, the Supreme Court would enhance national power.[60]

4. Republican Party Dominance

For several reasons, one must be careful not to surmise too much from partisan patterns surrounding the 1800 presidential election. The party system arose in the 1790s as an instrument of the political elite, not of the electoral masses. The system had just begun to organize. Its geographical scope was limited and its purpose originally understood as temporary. The opposing parties did, nevertheless, distinguish candidates along policy lines and effectively mobilize the electorate during the 1790s, the 1800 campaign, and beyond. Substantial evidence

---

[56]For a discussion of the extent to which *Hudson* addressed a tension between common law and the Constitution, *see* Gary D. Rowe, "The Sound of Silence: United States v. Hudson & Goodwin, Jeffersonian Ascendancy, and the Abolition of Federal Common Law Crimes, 101 *Yale Law Journal* 919 (1992).

[57]White, *The Jeffersonians*, p. 14; *but see* Banning, *The Jeffersonian Persuasion*, p. 279.

[58]10 U.S. (6 Cranch) 87 (1810).

[59]10 U.S. (6 Cranch) 87, 135 (1810).

[60]*See, e.g., Martin v. Hunter's Lessee*, 14 U.S. (1 Wheat.) 304 (1816) (holding that Supreme Court has appellate jurisdiction over state courts); *McCulloch v. Maryland*, 17 U.S. (4 Wheat.) 316 (1819) (finding congressional authority to incorporate a bank under the "necessary and proper" provision of the U.S. Constitution, art I, § 8).

regarding the strength of the changes effected by the Republicans beginning in 1800 therefore may be found in the degree of support the party received relative to the Federalists after 1800. Table I illustrates the point.

TABLE I*

Year	Pres. Electors Fed.	Rep.	House Members Fed.	Rep.	Senate Members Fed.	Rep.
1792	77ª	55ª	54	52	17	13
1794			48	57	19	13
1796	71	68	58	48	20	12
1798			63	43	19	13
1800	65	73	41	65	14	18
1802			39	102	9	25
1804	14	162	25	116	7	27
1806			24	118	6	28
1808	47	122	48	94	6	28
1810			36	108	6	30
1812	b	128	68	112	9	27
1814			65	117	11	25
1816	34	183	42	141	10	32
1818			27ᶜ	156	7ᶜ	35

*This chart and date are adapted from William Nisbet Chambers, *Political Parties in a New Nation* (New York: Oxford University Press, 1963), p. 182 (1963), which relies on data from Bureau of the Census, *Historical Statistics of the United States, Colonial Times to 1957* (Washington, D.C., 1960), corrected by later data, where available.

ᵇ Fusion of DeWitt Clinton Republican faction and Federalists: 8
ᶜ Local remnants of national party, "nominally Federalists."

CONCLUSIONS

On the basis of the preceding analysis, it seems nearly incontrovertible that in the 1790s and in 1800, Jefferson and his Democratic-Republicans campaigned on an ideology that, if fully implemented, would have effected an exhaustive transformation the political and economic terrain shaped by the Federalists in the first years of the republic. In these first years, the Federalists had begun commercializing the nation's political economy, strengthening the central government against state power, and pursuing a foreign policy favoring British interests, especially as opposed to French interests, which suggested perhaps a more aristocratic identity of the American republic.

Following the Jefferson victory in 1800, fundamental change in the American constitutional occurred and endured through most of the next two decades. In the spirit of civic virtue, the Republicans retrenched the expanded scope of the national government and repudiated much of Hamilton's economic program. Criticism of government was decriminalized, and political parties becomes accepted as legitimate electoral institutions. Central authority was curtailed, in part, by stripping the federal judiciary of much of its jurisdiction and reshaping the circuitry. The prospect of federal common law authority also faded. But the federal judiciary still managed to enhance national power to some degree. The despised national bank survived, moreover, and the "new" Republicans of the 1810s did pursue some economic policies favored by the Federalists in the 1790s.

3. THE CONSTITUTIONAL POLITICS OF JACKSON

Jefferson's "revolution" of 1800 proved to be modest in scope, but transformative. During the campaign, the Republicans had portrayed the Federalists as advocates of a larger, centralized government that would sponsor financial speculation and destroy the civic virtue that binds society. The national bank, in fact, symbolized Hamilton's vision of the American economic order and ranked high on the Federalist political agenda. Not only did Jefferson decide to retain the national bank, however, a Republican Congress would re-establish the national bank during the Jeffersonian era, in 1816. Congress, in support of yet another Hamiltonian measure, placed high tariffs on textile imports to protect new industries. Thus, while Jeffersonian orthodoxy endured long past Jefferson's tenure in office, after two full decades, its integrity was strained, if not compromised. In 1828, Andrew Jackson, the military hero and champion of the "common man," won the U.S. presidency and refashioned the orthodox meaning of American democracy. By conventional historical accounts, Jackson ushered in a new era in American politics.[1] The question for present purposes is whether Jackson's politics were constitutionally transformative in nature and how the outcomes compare with the political procedures for constitutional change intimated in Article V of the Constitution.

In this chapter, the "era of Jackson" will be subjected to the same test applied to the Jeffersonian "revolution." Initially, the question to be pursued is whether Jackson's candidacy and proposals as President

---

[1]See e.g., Arthur M. Schlesinger, Jr., *The Age of Jackson*, (Boston: Little, Brown & Company, 1950); Marvin Meyers, *The Jacksonian Persuasion: Politics & Belief*, (Stanford: Stanford University Press, 1960); *see also* Joseph L. Blau, ed., *Social Theories of Jacksonian Democracy: Representative Writings of the Period 1825-1850*, (New York: The Liberal Arts Press, 1954).

signaled potentially transformative change in public policy. To be examined here, specifically, are: 1) the state of the Jeffersonian orthodoxy in the 1820s, 2) Jackson's campaign ideology in the 1828 election, 3) Jackson's convictions regarding political economy as they took shape once in office, 4) his use of the Presidency in pursuit of his political agenda, and 5) how party politics was reorganized pursuant to Jackson's political successes. The next step is to examine whether Jackson's presidency results in long-term transformation of the American constitutional order. In consideration of changes to the American party system and the institutions of representative government following his presidency, we will find some marked informal change to the constitutional order, but the change was intended to protect and preserve the Jeffersonian vision of the American republic.

WERE THERE CONSTITUTIONALLY TRANSFORMATIVE PROPOSALS UNDERLYING THE 1828-32 REALIGNMENT?

The Constitutional Status Quo Ante

It had been established during Jefferson's presidency and affirmed in subsequent presidencies that the administrative capacities of the national government were constitutionally limited–so limited, in fact, that even a system of internal improvements, which seemed a good idea to many Republicans, was not within the power of Congress to enact without an empowering amendment to the Constitution.[2]   This aspect of the Jeffersonian view of the American constitutional order, in fact, may have been the single most important development in constitutional law at the time, given the opposite direction that the Federalists had been leading American government and the economy during the 1790s. But after 1812, Congress re-established the national bank, notwithstanding Jefferson's earlier decision to allow the national bank to stand merely because it already had been established. Congress also placed high tariffs on textile imports to protect new industries in the country. Both the bank and tariffs were originally Hamiltonian techniques of political economy.

---

[2]*See* Stephen Skowronek, *The Politics Presidents Make: Leadership from John Adams to George Bush* (Cambridge: Harvard University Press, 1993), p. 105.

As President, James Monroe attempted to strike a balance between the Jeffersonian view of limited national government and a national interest in internal improvements. Despite reminders of an earlier acquiescence on his part to the limited administrative capacities view of the national government, Monroe as president sought middle ground, advancing the proposition that the national government legitimately could allocate the monies for internal improvements and offer them to states to use toward their allocated purposes.[3]

It was President John Quincy Adams who proposed policy initiatives that strained the Republican philosophy of government beyond its previously understood limits. Aiming to discard party labels and to run government on the basis of merit alone, Adams offered each of his rivals for the Presidency, including Andrew Jackson, a place in his new administration, and proceeded to advocate a sweeping national program of governance. He proposed a federal department of the interior, a national naval academy, a national university, a national astronomical observatory, a national bankruptcy law, a national militia law, a national system of weights and measures, a national patent law, and a national system of improvements and transportation. In Adams's eyes, the constitutional limitations that had constrained Monroe necessarily were dissolved by the benefits of this national program to "the people themselves."

> If these powers . . . may be effectively brought to action by laws promoting the improvement of agriculture, commerce and manufactures, the cultivation and encouragement of the mechanical arts, the advancement of literature, and the progress of the sciences, ornamental and profound, to refrain from exercising them for the benefit of the people themselves would be to hide in the earth the talent committed to our charge-- would be treachery to the most sacred of trusts.[4]

---

[3] *Id.*

[4] John Quincy Adams, December 6, 1925, *A Compilation of the Messages and Papers of the Presidents*, Vol. 2, ed. James D. Richardson (New York: Bureau of National Literature, 1897), pp. 881-882, as cited in Stephen Skowronek, *The*

The Adams administration, Skowronek reports, "projected a political departure more definitive than anything since 1801,"[5] and Adams' advisors made an effort to forge new political alliances supportive of the broad national program. From Skowronek's perspective, Adams failed in his effort to transform Republican ideology because of a failure to present a clear warrant for breaking with the tradition. He had touched a nerve among those concerned that government was becoming the foray for merely the ambitious and power-seeking, and did offer to preserve the "patrician principles of governmental management"[6] that had characterized the Republican era. His adaptation was to reify "talent and virtue" within the patrician context. But Adams could not undo the partisan activity that had been necessary in order to make him president in the election of 1824, in which there was no majority vote among presidential electors,[7] nor could he build a consensus for his program without creating partisans in its favor. Adams's break with Jeffersonian orthodoxy and his political ineptitude set the stage for Jackson's triumph in 1828.

As the Federalist party effectively came to an end by the early 1820s, the decade had began without a functional two-party system. But as Richard McCormick observes, "the stimulus for the formation of the second party system was supplied by the revival of the contest for the presidency in 1824 . . . The most important consequence of 1824, in terms of party formation, was that it projected Andrew Jackson to the fore as the rival to Adams."[8] The two candidates, McCormick explains,

---

Politics Presidents Make, p. 208.

[5]Skowronek, *The Politics Presidents Make*, p. 119.

[6]Skowronek's term, *see The Politics President's Make*, p. 121.

[7]*See id.*, p. 125.

[8]Richard P. McCormick, "Political Development and the Second Party System," in William Nisbet Chambers and Walter Dean Burnham, eds., *The American Party Systems: Stage of Political Development*, (New York: Oxford

appealed to voters along strongly sectional lines, continuing into the 1828 presidential election, too.

> [In 1828] Adams swept New England, securing majorities of three-to-one or better in favor of the six states. Jackson was equally impressive in the South, and won commanding majorities in most of the newer states of the West. Having no sectional candidate of their own in the race, the Middle States provided the major battleground of the election, and--except in Pennsylvania--the vote was extremely close. The party alignments that formed in the Middle States by 1828 tended to be durable . . ., although in both New York and Pennsylvania the anti-Jackson forces lacked cohesion and were distracted by Antimasonry. With these important exceptions, we could say that a new two-party system had emerged in the Middle States by 1828 and that it had been given definition by the presidential contest.[9]

McCormick notes, however, that after the 1828 election the alignments did not persist in the South and West. Clay's candidacy in the West in 1832 went nowhere; the South in 1832, with the exception of Kentucky, could be described as monolithically Jacksonian.[10]

But Jackson's presidency ultimately served as the catalyst for a new, structured two-party system. The new system would be crystallized following the "political explosion [that] rocked the South from Virginia to Mississippi in 1834 and 1835."[11] The end of Jackson's presidency destroyed the preexisting consensus he had sustained, creating cleavages in the old alignments that manifested in new party structures. As McCormick explains,

---

University Press, 1975), p. 97.

[9]*Id.*, p. 98-99.

[10]*Id.*, p. 99.

[11]*Id.*, p. 100.

With Jackson nearing the end of his tenure, the political consensus that seemingly had prevailed was abruptly replaced by a sharp cleavage in almost every state. Those who remained loyal to the Jackson party found themselves confronted with a virulent opposition that shared a common antagonism to [Jackson's hand-picked successor] Martin Van Buren. While some of those "antis" continued to profess their undying loyalty to Old Hickory and his policies, others declaimed against executive usurpation, the removal of bank deposits, and the tariff, or sounded the changes on states' rights. The new sides were drawn in the state and congressional elections of 1834 and 1835, and by 1836 the Southern opposition parties–often bearing the name Whig–had found their standard bearer in Hugh Lason White of Tennessee.[12]

In the West, too, Van Buren Democratic parties contested against opposition parties.

Constitutionally Transformative Electoral Issues:

1. Populist, Decentralized Political Economy

In neither the 1824 nor the 1828 presidential elections did Jackson present himself as a fundamentally transformative chief executive. He capitalized on his reputation as a hero of the 1812 war with Britain and, being of humble origins, marketed himself as an "ordinary man's" candidate. Beyond this image, he was known to advance only the following specific policy positions: 1) retirement of the national debt, 2) states rights, 3) "just" treatment of Native Americans, and 4) the "rotation" of appointed officials in government. None of these overtly represents an appeal for extraordinary departure from the politics of the regimes of the past.

Jackson's candidacy, however, takes on more potential importance in the context of developments in political economy at the time. As Congress proceeded to protect particular industries and sponsor internal

---

[12] *Id.*

improvements to some degree into the 1820s, concerns mounted regarding the danger that prosperity might pose for free institutions and republicanism. Particular groups opposed to these developments became visible. As Joseph Blau explains, among the lower middle class there emerged a collection of farmers and landowners who were taxed for roads and canals they neither needed nor wanted.[13] This group advocated "hard money" and therefore distrusted banks and banks' paper money. Artisans and master mechanics who resented the "head start" that protected industries were receiving also emerged, Blau adds.[14] In the South especially, "states rights" advocates, who feared that a concentration of power in the national government could lead to the eradication of slavery, emerged on the political scene.[15] Taxpayer suffrage, as George Tindall observes, had expanded across many states as a means for combating the rise of powerful commercial and manufacturing interests. "The spread of the suffrage," he explains, "brought a new type of politician to the fore, the man who had special appeal to the masses or knew how to organize the people for political purposes,"[16] a role Jackson fit well. As President, in fact, Jackson exerted considerable leverage against other political institutions or actors by manufacturing, or appealing to, popular opinion.[17]

As Jackson exerted this leverage, Jacksonian political philosophy became more defined, so that to be a Jacksonian would be to embrace classically liberal economics–and staunchly so. The Jacksonians, as Blau observes, "criticized Adam Smith for having admitted any economic

---

[13]Joseph Blau, ed., *Social Theories of Jacksonian Democracy, supra* n. 1, p. xiv.

[14]*Id.*

[15]*Id.*

[16]George Tindall, *America: A Narrative History*, vol. 1 (New York: W.W. Norton, 1983), p. 390.

[17]This is precisely what he does, beginning especially in 1832, as will be demonstrated in the next section of this chapter.

restrictions into his system."[18] But why be such advocates for liberal economics? From the Jacksonian perspective, liberal economics best promote the interests of "the real people"–farmers, planters, mechanics, and laborers.[19] These occupations are distinguished by their moral worth. Such laborers exhibit independent spirit, a love of liberty, intelligence, high moral character, and qualities that contribute to republicanism. As Meyers suggests, promotional, financial, and commercial pursuits are left out of the conception of "real." "The point seems to be," he explains,

> "that virtue naturally attaches to, and in fact takes much of its definition from, callings which involve some immediate, responsible function in the production of goods. . . . Defective morals, habits, and character are nurtured in the trades which seek wealth without labor, employing the strategems of speculative maneuver, privilege-grabbing, and monetary manipulation."[20]

As Meyers notes, such a belief regarding the sources of virtue and vice helps to explain Jackson's conception of wealth in a liberal economic order. Wealth inherently is neither good nor bad, and Jackson should not be understood as anti-wealth. What is of greatest concern for Jacksonian economics is how wealth is acquired. If it is acquired through "speculative maneuver, privilege-grabbing, and monetary manipulation," the those who hold it are suspect. This type of wealth is "money power."[21]

"Money power," moreover, was precisely Jackson's concern with the Bank of the United States. The bank, like other corporations, represented a concentration of wealth borne of financial manipulation and privilege.

---

[18]Blau, *Social Theories of Jacksonian Democracy*, p. xii.

[19]Marvin Meyers, *The Jacksonian Persuasion. Politics & Belief*, (Stanford: Stanford University Press, 1960), p. 21.

[20]*Id.*, p. 22.

[21]*Id.*, p. 52.

"[T]he Jacksonians," Meyers observes, "blamed the Bank for the transgressions committed by the people of their era against the political, social, and economic values of the Old Republic."[22] The Old Republic had not endorsed concentrations of wealth and had strongly limited administrative capacities at the national level.

2. Plebiscitary Partisanship

As an attempt to establish an enduring means for combating privilege extracted through government, Jackson also advanced the substitution of more participatory party structures for the traditional rule by a patrician elite. This measure followed a congressional rejection of several of his early requests for policy and institutional reform, even after he had attempted to govern by consensus.

In his first message to the United States Congress, Jackson proposed that the Constitution be amended to remove the House of Representatives from the process of selecting a winner in presidential election runoff contests, and to limit presidents to one term of office. He also attacked the entrenchment of many administrative personnel.[23] Yet following this "order-shattering" initial message, as Skowronek observes, Jackson appeared more moderate. Jackson expressed a willingness to work with his opposition and to keep the federal government involved in the provision of public works, at least to some degree. With regard to the national bank, Jackson, throughout most of his first term of office, merely suggested reforming it so as to remedy the constitutional difficulties in its preexisting design.[24] And Jackson, to the surprise and dismay of Senator John Calhoun, even rejected South Carolina's attempted nullification of federal tariff policy as it applied to South Carolina.

---

[22]*Id.*, p. 11.

[23]Jackson's plan for "rotation" of appointments in theory and practice is discussed in Leonard D. White, *The Jacksonians: A Study in Administrative History, 1829-1861*, (New York: Macmillan, 1956).

[24]Skowronek, *The Politics Presidents Make*, p. 136.

This rift is illuminating. The break between Calhoun and Jackson, Skowronek observes, "is especially instructive in showing how the patrician mode of governance was displaced and a new one less dependent on personal deference formed in its stead."[25] Unable to trust Calhoun, Jackson was forced to be less consensual and to utilize more party-led tactics in his leadership. The Senate rejected some of Jackson's appointments for a more representative bureaucracy, and the House expressed confidence in the preexisting banking system. In the context of his Indian removal bill, Skowronek explains, Jackson "began to organize a congressional party identified with presidential leadership."[26] Defeated opponents noted the significance of this measure, charging it with "executive despotism" and advanced anti-Jacksonian themes that served as a basis for an alternative party, the Whigs.

Jackson then vetoed several internal improvements projects, explaining that he remained open to such measures but also was concerned about the various interests of the states. His solution was subsidies to the states, the position Monroe previously had taken on the issue of the scope of federal government administrative authority. According to Skowronek, Jackson's change of plans here signaled his intent to achieve reform on his own terms, and that, as of mid-1831, "the President was still able to act on these intentions while cultivating a broad middle ground between nullification and nationalization . . ."[27] Jackson, in fact, tried to remain a consensus leader by also acknowledging threats to states rights posed by his plan to redistribute surplus revenues and by separating tariff reform "from any implied institutionalization of a state interest in protection."[28]

3. *Expanded Legislative Authority of the President*

---

[25] *Id.*

[26] *Id.*, p. 139.

[27] *Id.*, p. 140.

[28] *Id.*, p. 140.

In the last year of Jackson's first term, the House and Senate voted to re-charter the national bank without any substantial effort to accommodate Jackson's concerns. Jackson responded in ways that would help to define him ideologically and that would serve to redefine the governing constitutional order. At the time, the only legitimate ground for a presidential veto of congressional legislation was understood to be constitutionality. In 1819, the Supreme Court had decided that a national bank was constitutional.[29] Under the Jeffersonian orthodoxy, moreover, the executive was to defer to the legislature, as Jefferson himself generally had done following his campaign against Federalist excesses. But Jackson vetoed the re-charter bill, and in his veto message repudiated two elements of the previous constitutional order–executive deference to either the Supreme Court or Congress on matters of constitutionality, and executive deference to legislation affecting the executive branch. Skowronek explains:

> Jackson not only reaffirmed his initial assertion that the Bank had failed in its mission; he renounced the assumption of executive deference to the Court on questions of constitutionality. Then, turning to the question of executive deference to Congress, he claimed that the Bank was an agency of the executive branch, and he asserted a presidential prerogative over legislative action that affected that branch. On both sides, Jackson pressed the case for the equality of the branches. "The opinion of the judges has no more authority over Congress than the opinion of Congress has over the judges, and on that point, the President is independent of both."[30]

Linking the bank to the unscrupulous aggrandizement of power at the expense of the great majority, Jackson came to repudiate the institutional arrangements that would preserve an order tainted by a "conspiracy of power, privilege, and self-interest."

That Jackson would take these steps just prior to the 1832 election,

---

[29] *McCulloch v. Maryland*, 17 U.S. (4 Wheat) 316 (1819).

[30] Skowronek, *The Politics Presidents Make*, p. 142.

moreover, allowed him to take his case to "the people themselves." His veto message was offered "as a political manifesto for popular judgment," Skowronek observes.[31] In Jackson's own words:

> A general discussion will now take place, eliciting new light and settling important principles; and a new Congress, elected in the midst of such discussion . . . will bear to the Capitol the verdict of public opinion.[32]

Jackson won re-election triumphantly. But a renewed challenge to his authority would force continued struggle over the revised constitutional order he aimed to fashion. Just as Jackson was re-elected, South Carolina reignited the federal-states relations issue by officially nullifying the 1828 and 1832 tariff acts and threatened to secede from the Union, if federal authority were invoked to enforce the acts. Jackson, of course, earlier had rejected nullification, and now resolved to quash this challenge to his authority, despite his own commitment to the states' rights aspect of Jeffersonian orthodoxy. Jackson, as Skowronek observes, took the substance of South Carolina's grievance as his own and proceeded to abandon federal protections, oppose the use of public land for the support of national projects, call for the disposal of all federal stock in private corporations, and, ignoring the Supreme Court's ruling against Georgia regarding the rights of Cherokee,[33] demanded that his removal plan for the Cherokee be respected.[34] Jackson then issued a forceful proclamation declaring the power of a state to annul a law of the United States "incompatible with the existence of the Union, contradicted expressly by the letter of the Constitution, [and] unauthorized by its

---

[31]*Id.*, p. 144.

[32]Quoted in Skowronek, p. 144. *See also* Veto Message, July 10, 1832, in James D. Richardson, ed., *A Compilation of the Messages and Papers of the Presidents, 1789-1897*, 10 vols. (Washington: U.S. Government Printing Office, 1896-1899), vol 2, p. 582.

[33]*Worcester v. Georgia*, 31 U.S. (5 Pet.) 515 (1832).

[34]*See* Skowronek, *The Politics Presidents Make*, p. 145.

spirit, inconsistent with every principle on which it was founded, and destructive of the great object for which it was formed."[35] He followed up this pronouncement with a proposal to Congress that he be granted the power to use federal troops preemptively in South Carolina to enforce federal law. Jackson's action on tariffs and public works and his action on nullification, Skowronek suggests, were calculated to forge another grand coalition, but instead they served to alienate both the states' rights camp and strong Union supporters.

Amid these actions, with his own re-election as the asserted basis for authority, Jackson decided to remove federal deposits from the national bank and place them in preferred state banks. In the 1832 election the people spoke on the bank issue, he explained, so the question was decided. In the spring of 1833, Jackson selected bank-opponent William Duane for Treasury Secretary, with the expectation that Duane would remove the federal deposits from the bank. Duane, however, ultimately expressed reservations about the president's authority in this matter, given that, by law, the treasury had a special relationship to Congress and some independence from the President. Jackson dismissed Duane and replaced him with Roger Taney, who carried out the task, and who, upon Federalist Chief Justice John Marshall's death in 1835, would be appointed the new Chief Justice on the Court. Jackson was censured by the Senate for abusing his power to accomplish removal of the federal deposits.

4. Balance of Power Between the Federal Government and the States

The Supreme Court's exercise of judicial review during or following critical electoral periods may illuminate which particular aspects of the constitutional order are being challenged by transformative politics; some attention to Supreme Court decisions in a previous electoral order may give some perspective on why. In the context of the 1828 realignment, an inquiry into federal court opinions reveals that issues of federal-state relations increasingly reached the Supreme Court.

It is well-established that the Supreme Court, while under the

---

[35]*Id.*, p. 146.

leadership of the Federalist Chief Justice Marshall, which lasted for the duration of the Jeffersonian era, issued rulings that often limited state autonomy and expanded federal authority, despite Jeffersonian orthodoxy.[36] The Court, for example, had determined that Article III of the Constitution authorizes federal courts to review state court decisions regarding federal law.[37] In 1819, in *McCulloch v. Maryland*,[38] Marshall reasoned that Congress, under both the express and implied powers granted by the Constitution, possesses the authority to charter a national bank, and that in cases in which state and national interests conflict, national interests must prevail. On the basis of the contract clause of the Constitution,[39] the Court also had prohibited a state from discharging debts contracted before the enactment of an insolvency law.[40]

The reach of the federal government pursuant to the interstate commerce clause also was expanded, but with particular limits. In 1824, in *Gibbons v. Ogden*,[41] the Supreme Court held that Gibbons's federal license to operate a steamboat gave him a right to operate his boats across the Hudson River between New York and New Jersey, notwithstanding a state law to the contrary. *Gibbons*, as David Currie observes, marked "the beginning of incessant litigation over the extent to which state

---

[36]For discussion, *see* Robert G. McCloskey, *The American Supreme Court*, 2nd ed. (Chicago: The University of Chicago Press, 1994), or David P. Currie, *The Constitution in the Supreme Court: The First Hundred Years 1789-1888*, (Chicago: The University of Chicago Press, 1985).

[37]*Martin v. Hunter's Lessee*, 14 U.S. (1 Wheat.) 304 (1816).

[38]17 U.S. (4 Wheat.) 316 (1819).

[39]U.S. Const., art. I, § 10.

[40]*Sturges v. Crowninshield*, 17 U.S. (4 Wheat.) 122 (1819).

[41]22 U.S. (9 Wheat.) 1 (1824).

legislation is precluded by the commerce clause."[42] The issue of exclusivity of various grants of federal power had been broached earlier by the Supreme Court, and at no point had the Marshall Court reasoned that a grant of federal authority was exclusive, even when an opportunity to do so might have been relatively incontrovertible.[43] But the Marshall Court, in 1827, struck down a Maryland law imposing a fee on imported goods to be sold, in consideration of both the Article I, section 10 prohibition of state taxes on imports without congressional consent and a reading of the commerce clause as the very authorization for importation into the United States.[44] Perhaps surprisingly, the Court in *Wilson v. Black Bird Creek Marsh Co.*[45], decided in 1829, upheld a state law that authorized construction of a dam obstructing a navigable creek, in light of dormant federal commerce clause authority on this matter. In 1832, in *Worcester v. Georgia*[46], the Court found Georgia's law regulating Indian affairs to be in violation of pre-existing treaties and federal authority to regulate commerce with Indian tribes, and precluded by exclusive federal authority to regulate relations between the United States and the Cherokee nation.

DID ANY TRANSFORMATIVE INITIATIVES HAVE WIDESPREAD SUPPORT BEYOND THE REALIGNING ERA?

Were Jackson's efforts as a popular tribune for reform of a constitutional order that he claimed was protecting the interests of a

---

[42]David P. Currie, *The Constitution in the Supreme Court: The First Hundred Years, 1789-1888*, (Chicago: The University of Chicago Press, 1985), p. 173.

[43]Currie, *supra*, points out that, in light of constitutional provisions, the Court could have reasoned that congressional power over bankruptcy and naturalization is exclusive, but in both *Sturges v. Crowninshield*, 17 U.S. (4 Wheat.) 1 (1820) and *Chirac v. Chirac*, 15 U.S. (2 Wheat.) 259 (1817), respectively, it did not.

[44]*Brown v. Maryland*, 25 U.S. (12 Wheat.) 419 (1827).

[45]27 U.S. (2 Pet.) 245 (1829).

[46]31 U.S. (6 Pet.) 515 (1832).

privileged elite met with a sufficient degree of popular support over time? Looking at the partisan equilibrium following Jackson's presidency, Supreme Court decisions on federal-state relations in this era, and the presidency, too, in this era, the answer seems an unequivocal yes. Jackson's advancement of laissez faire economics also was successful, especially at the national level, but it had an ironic and countervailing result.

1. A Populist, Decentralized Political Economy

–On the National Bank

The national bank represented the core of what Jacksonian political economy opposed, the alliance of government and business, and, as noted earlier, Jackson ultimately proposed to destroy this "monster" by removing federal government deposits in the bank and placing them in politically preferred state banks. As a calculated response to Jackson's removal plan, bank president Nicholas Biddle curtailed bank loans, intending to underscore the relevance of the bank for the nation's financial stability. The action, however, resulted in a nation-wide financial panic that Jackson could blame exclusively on the actions of the bank, and Jackson ultimately prevailed in his effort to destroy the bank, which effectively reversed the judgment of the Supreme Court in *McCulloch v. Maryland*.

Yet Jackson's success in the "bank war" created new and ironic difficulties for those of his persuasion: The deposit of funds in state banks expanded credit and created a speculative boom. What to do with the growing federal surplus, moreover, became a dilemma. Distributing the money to the states would further the speculative boom, through the creation of incentives for more internal improvements. If the federal government were to keep the money, it would have to be regulated. Jackson moved toward a "hard money" policy as a solution. His "specie circular" executive order in 1836 aimed to reduce speculation in the economy.

The Democratic Party became strongly divided over the matter of fiscal policy. The bank panic of 1837 ended the speculation boom, but, into the 1840s, the country experienced an economic depression. Some

Democrats blamed the problem on Jackson's destruction of the national bank, which encouraged the speculation boom, followed by his specie requirement, which curtailed credit. In 1840, nevertheless, Van Buren secured passage of the Independent Treasury Act, which locked federal funds in independent federal sub-treasuries insulated from the banking community.

But "[w]hat the Jackson mentality could not foresee," Tindall explains, "was the degree to which, in a growing country, unrestrained enterprise could lead on to new economic combinations, centers of gigantic power largely independent of governmental regulation."[47] The banking system continued to integrate. "[T]he ultimate irony would be that the laissez faire rationale for republican simplicity eventually became the justification for the growth of unregulated centers of economic power far greater than any ever wielded by Biddle's bank."[48]

–Federal-State Relations

Even though business and government continued to commingle after Jackson's tenure, his interest in limited federal authority in relation to state authority was moderately served by the Supreme Court, following Jackson's appointment of Roger Taney as Chief Justice and other appointments to the Court by Van Buren. As David Currie observes, "The new era opened with a bang in 1837 . . ." Three postponed cases concerning limitations on state power, *New York v. Miln*,[49] *Briscoe v.*

---

[47]George Tindall, *America: A Narrative History*, vol. 1, (New York: W.W. Norton, 1983), p.423.

[48]*Id*. For details on the growth of the banking system in this era, *see* Bray Hammond, *Banks and Politics in America from the Revolution to the Civil War* (Princeton: Princeton University Press, 1957).

[49]36 U.S. (11 Pet.) 102 (1837).

Bank of Kentucky,[50] and *Charles River Bridge v. Warren Bridge*,[51] were decided by the Court. In each case, the Court upheld state authority, with a dissenting Justice Joseph Story "lamenting the dismantling of all that Marshall had built" in each. But ultimately, it should be noted, "the Taney Court did not take a narrow view of Congress's commerce power."[52]

New York v. Miln involved the constitutionality of a New York statute aimed at preventing immigrants from becoming public charges by requiring ship captains to furnish local authorities with a list of all passengers brought into the state. Writing for the Court, Justice Philip Barbour observed that it already been established that states could constitutionally respect commerce in the exercise of police powers and reasoned that the statute in question similarly aims to protect the public welfare.[53] *Briscoe v. Bank of Kentucky* involved the constitutionality of a negotiable instrument issued by a state bank, in light of the Constitution's provision in article I, section 10 against state bills of credit. In his majority opinion, Justice John McLean reasons that the instruments to which the Framers objected were those issued on the credit of the state, but the instrument in question here was issued on the credit of the bank. Unlike the state, the bank here could be sued without its consent, and all its assets could be seized to satisfy the obligation; the credit of the state thus is not significantly implicated.[54] In *Charles River Bridge v. Warren Bridge*, the Supreme Court affirmed a state court decision that an 1828 charter issued by the Massachusetts legislature for the construction of a bridge adjacent to an earlier-constructed bridge did not impair the obligation of a 1785 charter issued by the state for the first bridge. Writing for the majority, Chief Justice Taney reasoned that the

---

[50]36 U.S. (11 Pet.) 257 (1837).

[51]36 U.S. (11 Pet.) 420 (1837).

[52]David P. Currie, *The Constitution in the Supreme Court*, p. 234.

[53]36 U.S. (11 Pet.) 102, 139-41

[54]36 U.S. (11 Pet.) 257, 319-27.

only question is whether the state had promised not to build a bridge in the controversial location, and that the question could be answered by the common-law rule of construction for public grants, which resolves any ambiguity in favor of the public.[55]

But in 1843, the Supreme Court decided the first major contract clause case since Charles River Bridge, *Bronson v. Kinzie*,[56] and ruled against a state. At issue were Illinois statutes forbidding foreclosure sales for less than two-thirds of market value and allowing a mortgagor and his judgment creditors the right to redeem within a year after sale. With Chief Justice Taney writing for the majority, the Supreme Court held that both statutes violated the contract clause. In subsequent contract clause cases, the Court continued to protect interests under the clause.[57]

The most definitive statement by the Taney Court on the scope of federal commerce authority vis-a-vis state authority came in 1852 in *Cooley v. Board of Wardens*.[58] The case involved the legitimacy of a Pennsylvania law penalizing ships leaving port without local pilots. Writing for the majority, Justice Benjamin Curtis advanced a view of commerce clause authority under the Constitution squaring perfectly with the dual sovereignty ethic of Jackson. All matters of commerce that are national in nature, or that require uniform treatment are under the exclusive purview of Congress. If Congress has not exercised its power over commerce, states may exercise their own; and thus matters local in

---

[55]36 U.S. (11 Pet.) 420, 544-53.

[56]42 U.S. (1 How.) 311 (1843).

[57]*See, e.g., Gelpcke v. Dubuqune*, 68 U.S. (1 Wall.) 175 (1864) (holding for bondholders seeking recovery of interest following state court's declaration of illegitimacy of bond issue after initially authorizing the issue); *see also The Passenger Cases*, 48 U.S. (7 How.) 283 (1849) (declaring void New York and Massachusetts fees on ship captains for every passenger brought into the states).

[58]53 U.S. (12 How.) 299 (1852).

nature may be regulated by local authorities.[59]

As Currie explains, "*Cooley* began a new era, but practically speaking it concluded the Taney Court's pronouncements on the negative effect of the commerce clause." In several instances, in fact, it proceeded to protect interstate commerce from state interference.[60]

2. Plebiscitary Partisanship

Jackson had been critical of governmental structures that reduced to rule exclusively by the patrician order, and during his administration helped to form a party structure less tied to the patrician elite. This move was an effort to protect his presidential power, but, as McCormick observes, the first party system in the United States, the Jeffersonian Republicans and the Federalists, also had centered largely on presidential elections.[61] In the first party system, in fact, the caucus was the primary instrument for party development, and the congressional caucus was the primary vehicle for selecting presidential candidates. But in the second party system, ushered into existence by the politics of Andrew Jackson, "the caucus was almost completely replaced by the convention as the characteristic device for party management,"[62] reflecting, in part, increased demand for popular participation in party affairs.

This new connection between parties and the electorate would mean a new complexity in the organization of parties. McCormick reports:

> The widespread adoption of the convention system in the 1830s, with its hierarchy of delegate conventions and party committees extending from the smallest electoral unit up to the national

---

[59]53 U.S. (12 How) at 318.

[60]*See* Currie, *supra*, n. 12, p. 235.

[61]Richard McCormick, "Political Development and the Second Party System," *supra*, n. 8, p. 104.

[62]*Id.*, p. 105.

conventions, made for an exceedingly elaborate and complex organizational structure. Because candidates had to be nominated at so very many different levels of government, elections were held so frequently, and the party system embraced the entire range of offices, the organizations that had evolved in most states by the 1840s were marvels of ingenuity and intricacy and required enormous manpower to staff them. In contrast to the diversity of organizational forms under the first party system, there was now a high degree of uniformity throughout the nation and in both major parties.[63]

Such complex organization of the two-party system exists to this day in the United States.

As president, Jackson had cited his electoral victory as authority for his campaign against the bank, and another enduring change in the electoral system following his presidency was the move to the popular, at-large election of presidential electors.[64] This development gave a popular dimension to the contest for the presidency, reduced the political authority of the state legislatures, called forth elaborate and intensive campaign efforts, facilitated the building of national parties, reduced the effectiveness of third parties, and made the presidential election the focal point of the party system–to suggest but a few consequences.[65]

3. Legislative Capacity of the President

In regard to the authority of the President in relation to Congress, only some of Jackson's actions were sustained for an appreciable length of time. Jackson claimed the right of the Chief Executive to veto legislation on grounds other than constitutionality, and this practice has survived to the present. Jackson also expanded the policy making authority of the executive office by successfully preventing South Carolina's nullification

---

[63]*Id.*, pp. 105-06.

[64]*Id.*, p. 110.

[65]*Id.*, pp. 110-11.

of the federal tariff.

But Jackson's assertions during the bank war, that the opinion of the Supreme Court is binding neither on the President nor Congress, and that the executive does not function simply to carry out the will of the legislature, were less well-respected over time. Presidential restraint characterized each of the remaining nineteenth-century presidencies, except for those of James Polk and Abraham Lincoln. And Jackson's choice for Chief Justice, Roger Taney, would vehemently declare the Missouri Compromise unconstitutional in *Dred Scott v. Sanford*[66] in 1857, which either belies the credibility of Jackson's position on the non-binding character of Court opinions or makes Taney's opinion intended as mere "observation," the latter not fitting with the historical record. It should be noted, moreover, that Jackson's call for removal of the House of Representatives from participation in presidential runoff elections and one-term presidencies was not respected, and, in the case of one-term presidencies, not even by Jackson.

CONCLUSIONS

Jackson, as both presidential candidate and President, led a constitutionally transformative campaign, and he left a constitutional legacy. As a presidential candidate, Jackson presented himself as a popular tribune, determined to liberate the national government from the hold of a privileged class of individuals who had achieved their status by manipulating the national government pursuant to their interests. Once in office, Jackson successfully repudiated much of the expansion in federal administrative capacities,[67] including congressional authority to charter a national bank, although the laissez faire economics that he championed failed as a means of preserving a "chaste" republican order.

---

[66] 60 U.S. (19 How.) 393 (1857).

[67] White reports, in fact, that "[f]ormer attitudes about public expenditures, dominant especially among the old Republicans, persisted during the Jacksonian years. Spending the taxpayers' money was tinged with a sense of sin, and the less that could be spent the better, except where some local or party benefit was apparent." White, *The Jacksonians*, p. 154.

In terms of presidential authority, Jackson expanded the policy making capacity of the Chief Executive and secured the legitimacy of a presidential veto on grounds other than constitutionality. Federal-state relations continued to be contentious after Jackson's presidency, but Supreme Court decisions affirmed the authority of states in the federal system somewhat more firmly than Marshall Court opinions had done in the previous era.

Jackson's presidency also helped to establish a new party system, one fundamentally more democratic than the previous system. Jackson did not win the presidency in 1824, but his candidacy, with Adams as his opposition, helped to establish political alignments along sectional lines in much of the country. By 1828, with Jackson running for president again, these alignments were solidified. Defeats in Congress led Jackson to organize a congressional party and move away from government by consensus of elites toward more toward party-led government. Ultimately Jackson would appeal to the electorate for judgment on his actions and to their support as a mandate for his authority. His actions pursuant to this conception of authority, particularly in regard to the national bank and the South Carolina nullification crises, contributed to the organization of an opposition party, the Whigs.

Ultimately it was the presidential election of 1836, McCormick observes, that "was of crucial importance in determining the ultimate outlines of the second party system."[68] "In marked contrast to the situation that had existed in 1832, there were now two parties contesting elections in every state, and–no less significantly–in the large majority of the states the parties were competitive."[69] "[T]he effect of Van Buren's candidacy [in 1836]," McCormick adds, "was to end the monolithic character of Southern politics and delineate and strengthen alignments in the West, thereby giving a truly national dimension to the second party system. This new party system embraced the development of more democratic party structures and the popular, at-large, election of presidential electors.

---

[68]*Id.*, p. 101.

[69]*Id.*

4. EQUALITY, ECONOMICS, AND FEDERAL AUTHORITY IN THE POST-1850s

In terms of whether it signaled prospective constitutional transformation, the 1850s realignment is deceptively easy to assess. A few years following the collapse of the Whig party and the formation of the Republican party, the Civil War would erupt over the fundamental–and at this point longstanding–issue of state autonomy in relation to federal authority, and the Union victory in the war would be memorialized by three formal amendments to the U. S. Constitution. But the matter is not so easily dispatched for three reasons. First, the electoral crisis that began in the mid-1850s manifests in civil war before a stable electoral pattern returns in the 1870s, making particular political developments during and after the war potentially transformative measures. Second, given the exclusion of southern delegations from Congress at the time of the proposal of both the Thirteenth and Fourteenth Amendments to the Constitution, and the requirement of their ratification by the excluded states before these states would be readmitted to Congress, the textual requirements of the amendment provision of the Constitution, Article V, seem not to have been followed, in a strict sense, making the processes that were followed enormously important for the matter of the legitimacy of these amendments. Third, there has been enormous debate over the "original intent" of the Civil War Amendments, because of the pivotal role they have played, particularly the Fourteenth, in the expansion of both federal government authority and the federal protection of individual rights in the twentieth century, and an investigation of the processes surrounding their ratification might yield some interpretive insight relevant to both the post-1868 era and contemporary debates on the Amendment.

The investigation here again will focus on two major questions for legitimacy during this moment of electoral upheaval: 1) whether the realignment of the 1850s was premised on transformative public policy, and 2) whether any transformative outcomes were sustained by widespread approval. Part I of the chapter examines the first question. Unlike the previous two chapters, an inquiry into judicial review in this period will not be separated in any way from a review of potentially transformative public policy. The fundamental importance of judicial review to issue processing in this era allows this discussion to be integrated fully into the discussion of potentially transformative policy. Part II examines the question of precisely what emerged from this realignment with long-term, widespread support.

DO CONSTITUTIONALLY TRANSFORMATIVE PROPOSALS ANIMATE THE 1850s REALIGNMENT?

The Constitutional Status Quo Ante

By the 1850s, the bitter differences that had existed between the Democrats and the Whigs during Jackson's presidency, had faded to a considerable degree.[1] Sectionalism had posed the greatest danger to the American polity, but President Van Buren astutely gave permanence to the two-party system arising during Jackson's administration as a substitute for sectionalism.[2] In the years following, in fact, industrialization and the changes it wrought seem to have provided such political common ground that inter-party competition became almost difficult to sustain. The nation's territorial expansion of the late 1840s and early 1850s, however, would reactivate sectional issues.

With the prospective acquisition of territory from Mexico, in light of the U.S.-Mexico War, the vexing question of what authority the federal government possessed to restrict slavery in the territories was raised again. Fourteen states endorsed the Wilmot Proviso of 1846, which advocated the prohibition of slavery in new territories. The Proviso split both Whigs and Democrats, and helped a new party, the Free Soil Party, to coalesce around the anti-slavery position. In the 1848 presidential

---

[1]Michael F. Holt, *The Political Crisis of the 1850s*, (New York: Wiley, 1978), pp. 102-03.

[2]*Id.*, pp. 25-33.

election, the Free Soil Party split both the Democratic and the Whig votes, but the Whig Zachary Taylor prevailed, and the two traditional parties managed to survive at the national level. To the dismay of Southern Whigs, Taylor announced his belief in the legitimacy of slavery where it already existed, but also advocated quickly making California and New Mexico states, as a means of bypassing the question of whether slavery could exist in new territories. Following one of the great debates in the history of the U.S. Congress, the Compromise of 1850 was reached and, for a time, effected a settlement of the issue. The elements of the Compromise, which was proposed by Henry Clay, were to admit California as a free state, make no restriction regarding slavery on the rest of the Southwest, limit Texas's claim to a boundary to the source of the Rio Grande and compensate for this by assuming the Texas debt, uphold slavery in the District of Columbia but abolish slave trade in the District, adopt a fugitive slave act more favorable to slave-catchers, and preclude Congress from interfering with interstate slave trade.

Effective in the short-term, the Compromise on sectionalism would be exploded by sectional issues arising from the development of railroads and federal sponsorship of them, and from more territorial acquisition by the United States. Interest in railroad routes from the Mississippi River to the Pacific coast had grown considerably, and competition emerged for federal favor of particular routes. President Franklin Pierce recognized that the legitimacy of federal sponsorship of internal improvements was still questionable and urged caution before proceeding. Pierce also sought to expand the territory of the nation, seeking to purchase Cuba from Spain and more southwest territory from Mexico. But Pierce's appointment of James Gadsden as minister to Mexico for purposes of negotiating the acquisition of territory, as Skowronek observes, made territorial acquisition and the development of railroad routes "begin to work at cross purposes."[3]

Gadsden was a South Carolinian who actively had been seeking a southern rail route to the Pacific. Illinois Senator Stephen Douglas, however, had been seeking a northern rail route from Chicago to San Francisco, and Congress already had frustrated his efforts "by refusing to

---

[3]Stephen Skowronek, *The Politics Presidents Make*, p. 188.

organize a territorial government in the remaining portion of the old Louisiana Purchase through which it would have to pass,"[4] which was Nebraska territory. Because this Nebraska territory was still subject to the Missouri Compromise of 1820 and therefore closed to slavery, "the prospect of organizing free territory for the sake of the northern rail route was not the stuff to engage southern interests."[5] This sectional conflict over the parameters of railroad development set the stage for the reopening of the sectional issue. "In this circumstance," Skowronek explains, "Pierce's Mexican initiative left Douglas more anxious than ever to secure southern support for his Nebraska bill, and the heightened sensitivity to antislavery sentiments in the North made southerners more insistent that there could be no organization of the Nebraska territory without an explicit repeal of the Missouri Compromise."[6]

Constitutionally Transformative Issues:

1. Federal Authority to Restrict Slavery

In 1854, Douglas introduced a Nebraska bill that ultimately would ignite more debate over slavery than railroads. In order to gain southern support for his railroad plan, Douglas made concessions to slavery. His initial bill attempted to feign support of southern slavery, but he ultimately found it necessary to support an amendment to the bill that would repeal the Missouri Compromise, which for thirty-four years had kept sectional divisions at bay. Slavery now could become established in Kansas. Attempting to position himself as a consensus leader, Pierce supported the Kansas-Nebraska Act as a pro forma measure, in light of the Compromise of 1850, and the Act eventually passed. The strain of the Act, however, tore apart the Whig Party, and coalitions of independent Democrats, northern Whigs, and anti-slavery groups converged to form the Republican Party. In 1855, Pierce argued that the Kansas-Nebraska Act sustained a fundamental constitutional principle:

---

[4]*Id.*

[5]*Id.*

[6]*Id.*

"No portion of the United States shall undertake through the assumption of the powers of the General Government to dictate the social institutions of any other portion."[7]

In the 1856 presidential campaign, the Democratic Party platform endorsed the Kansas-Nebraska Act and reiterated that Congress should not have the authority to interfere with slavery in the states or territories. The Republicans ran John Fremont, and the party platform condemned both the repeal of the Missouri Compromise and slavery. It was, as Tindall observes, the first time a major party platform opposed slavery.[8] The American Party ran Millard Fillmore. Buchanan, of course, won.

In 1857, the *Dred Scott v. Sanford*[9] decision of the U.S. Supreme Court effectively declared the Republican program unconstitutional. Writing for the majority, Chief Justice Roger Taney reasoned that Scott, a Virginian slave who had been taken to free Illinois and Wisconsin Territory and thus was claiming to have been made free, could not bring suit because he was not a citizen, either under federal or state law. Taney, in fact, announced that the Declaration of Independence observation that all men are endowed with certain unalienable rights did not then, or in 1857, apply to the Negro. Although he thus had dissolved the issue of federal authority to proscribe slavery, Taney proceeded to an analysis of the legitimacy of the Missouri Compromise. The Compromise, he reasoned, deprived citizens of their property in slaves, an act illegitimate under the Constitution. The Court, therefore, for the first time since *Marbury v. Madison*, declared federal legislation unconstitutional. The Republicans protested the decision.

2. *The Legitimacy of Secession from the Union*

---

[7]"Third Annual Message," December 31, 1855, in James E. Richardson, *A Compilation of Messages and Papers of Presidents*, vol. 7 (New York: Bureau of National Literature, 1897), pp. 2873-2883, cited in Skowronek, *The Politics Presidents Make*, p. 196.

[8]George Brown Tindall, *America: A Narrative History*, vol. 1, p. 597.

[9]60 U.S. (19 How.) 393 (1857).

The Republican Party gained national stature through the 1858 elections, in part by embracing the protective tariff and homestead issues.[10] In 1860, the Republicans nominated as their presidential candidate Abraham Lincoln, who had gained national prominence through his senatorial campaign debates with Stephen Douglas in 1858. The Republican platform affirmed the right of states to control and protect their domestic institutions but reiterated its position against the extension of slavery. With only 39 percent of the popular vote but a strong- majority electoral vote, Lincoln won the presidential election, winning all the free states. But shortly after the election, the South Carolina legislature assembled a special convention on the election. In consideration of the threats to slavery posed by the election of Lincoln, the convention approved an Ordinance of Secession, which declared South Carolina's ratification of the Constitution repealed and the union with other states dissolved. In February of 1861, seven southern states adopted a provision for the Confederate States of America. Compromise efforts in Congress were attempted until the time of Lincoln's inauguration, and the promise that slavery would be allowed where it already existed met with some success, though, as Tindall notes, many Republicans, including Lincoln, "were unwilling to repudiate their stand against slavery in the territories."[11] The compromise, nevertheless, passed both the House and Senate, and had it ever been ratified by the states, this proposed Thirteenth Amendment to the Constitution would have guaranteed, by name, "slavery."[12]

In the first years of Republican rule, nevertheless, both Congress and the President were notably conservative in their objectives for the Civil War. Lincoln initially prosecuted the war only with the objective of keeping the Union together. As J.G. Randall observes, in the first stages of the Civil War, the administration was committed to a policy of "non-

---

[10]James Sundquist, *The Dynamics of the Party System: Alignment and Realignment of Political Parties in the United States* rev ed., (Washington: Brookings Institution, 1983), p. 82.

[11]Tindall, *America: A Narrative History*, vol. 1., p. 615.

[12]*Id.*, p. 616.

interference" with regard to slavery, with Lincoln in his inaugural address already repeating this position.[13] Congress had seemed to take the same position in solidly endorsing the Crittenden resolution of July 22, 1861, which declared that the war has nothing to do with interference in established institutions of the states.[14] In 1862, however, Congress and the President moved closer toward a general policy of emancipation. In April of that year, slavery in the District of Columbia was abolished. In the same month, Congress and the President proposed financial assistance to states that abolished slavery, although the plan was never carried out.[15] In June of the same year, emancipation in the federal territories was implemented. In September of 1863, Lincoln finally issued the Emancipation Proclamation, but it did not apply universally within the Confederate states nor to the border states, nor did it intend an abandonment of the compensation idea. "The compensation scheme was his idea of the proper method for the permanent eradication of slavery, while the proclamation was a measure of partial application whose legal effect after the war he regarded as doubtful."[16]

Further evidence of Lincoln's conservatism on the federal-state relations issue is found both in the contours of his plan for reconstruction of the South after the war and the selection of Andrew Johnson as Vice-President for the 1864 presidential election. Lincoln's premise for reconstruction was that the rebelling states remained a part of the Union; the actions to be punished were those of individuals leading the rebellion.[17] The basic contours of Lincoln's version of Reconstruction, as Eric Foner reports, issued on December 8, 1863, thus were as follows:

---

[13]J.G. Randall, *Constitutional Problems Under Lincoln*, rev. ed. (Glouster, Mass.: Peter Smith, 1963), p. 351.

[14]*Id.*, p. 352.

[15]See Randall, *Constitutional Problems Under Lincoln*, pp. 365-66.

[16]*Id.*, p. 367.

[17]*Id.*, pp. 48-73.

[The] Proclamation of Amnesty and Reconstruction offered full pardon and the restoration of rights "except as to slaves" to persons who resumed their allegiance by taking an oath of future loyalty, and pledged to accept the abolition of slavery. A few groups, including high ranking civil and military officers of the Confederacy, were excluded. When in any state the number of loyal Southerners, thus defined, amounted to 10 percent of the votes cast in 1860, this minority could establish a new state government. Its constitution must abolish slavery, but it could adopt temporary measures regarding blacks "consistent . . . with their present condition as a laboring, landless, and homeless class." Such a government would then be entitled to representation at Washington, although Lincoln was careful to note that each House of Congress retained the authority to judge the qualifications of its own members.[18]

Andrew Johnson secured the vice-presidential nomination in 1864, after having repudiated his own Tennessee's secession and having subsequently remained in his U.S. Senate seat. He, in fact, served on the congressional Committee on the Conduct of the War.[19] Kenneth Stamp fittingly assesses Johnson as a "Jacksonian", a southerner committed to the Union and intolerant of southern rebellion.[20]

3. Unilateral Military Power of the Executive

Following the Confederate attack on federal troops at Fort Sumter in April of 1861, but before Congress convened in July of that year, Lincoln unilaterally prosecuted the war against the Confederacy. In the process, at least three of his actions challenged the conventional understanding of the President's authority. First, Lincoln called for enlistments in the

---

[18]Eric Foner, *Reconstruction: America's Unfinished Revolution, 1863-1877,* (New York: Harper & Row, 1988), pp. 35-36.

[19]Kenneth M. Stampp, *The Era of Reconstruction, 1865-1877,* (New York: Alfred A. Knopf, 1982), p. 51.

[20]*See id.,* pp. 50-82.

regular army beyond the legal limit. Second, he suspended the habeas corpus privilege for captured Confederate troops. Third, he blockaded southern ports and seized particular ships that had violated the blockade. Over the course of the war, Lincoln also established martial law in particular sections of the country. Pursuant to Lincoln's martial law orders, military commissions were sometimes used to try civilians for offenses.[21]

4. National, Administrative Political Economy

The withdrawal of secessionist legislators from Congress allowed Republicans domineering control of Congress, resulting in fundamental departures from the Jacksonian and Jeffersonian political economy models of the American republic. Jefferson had established that the administrative capacities of the national government were constitutionally limited. Believing that the commitment to Jeffersonian orthodoxy had wavered by the 1820s, Jackson dismantled the national banking system and protective tariffs and successfully forged an ethic against government sponsorship of business or regulation of the economy. But before the end of 1862, a national banking act, a protective tariff, and a homestead act all were passed by Congress. The banking system established in 1863 and 1864 resulted in a uniform national currency that replaced various issues by banks. Banks formed under the National Banking Act also were required to issue bonds as means for financing the war. Higher taxes also were needed to finance the war, and, in 1862, Congress created the Bureau of Internal Revenue to collect the new revenue. The Homestead Act of 1862 offered citizens 160 acres of the public domain after five years of continuous residence. In the same year, the national government created the Department of Agriculture and passed the Morrill Act, which gave tracts of the public domain for the endowment of agricultural, or land grant, colleges. The national government also found it necessary to subsidize the development of, and to regulate, railroads.

The transformative nature of these Union policy developments may be

---

[21]For details on these measures, see the entirety of J.G. Randall, *Constitutional Problems Under Lincoln*, *supra*, n. 13.

seen in Andrew Johnson's resistance to them. Johnson, who claimed to have remained a Democrat, sharply criticized the Federalist political-economy developments engineered by the Republicans:

> . . . Johnson also made it clear that he regarded the protective tariff as an unjust burden upon consumers; the national banking system as a dangerous monopoly; and the sale of timber and mineral lands from the public domain to private corporations as a betrayal of the homestead policy adopted in 1862. "The public domain," he said, "is a national trust, set apart and held for the general welfare upon principles of equal justice, and not to be bestowed as a special privilege upon a favored class." In pure Jacksonian rhetoric, he denounced those who sought to obtain special favors from government. "Monopolies, perpetuities, and class legislation," he insisted, "are contrary to the genius of free government. . . . Wherever monopoly attains a foothold, it is sure to be a source of danger, discord, and trouble. . . ."[22]

After the war, Stampp reports, Johnson particularly was concerned about the public securities now held by many. "The aristocracy based on $3,000,000,000 of property in slaves . . . has disappeared; but an aristocracy based on over $2,500,000,000 of national securities, has arisen in the Northern states . . ."[23]

4. Political and Social Equality for Black Men--The Thirteenth Amendment

When the Civil War had begun, Lincoln's and the Republican Party's disdain for the institution of slavery was well-known. But the Republicans had tried to avert southern secession by agreeing to leave slavery alone in the states where it already existed. He respected the southern argument that Congress did not have the authority, at least in times of peace, to abolish slavery in the states. He, in fact, went to some

---

[22]*Id.*, p. 58.

[23]Johnson as quoted in Kenneth Stampp, *The Era of Reconstruction, 1865-1877*, p. 57.

lengths to explain that emancipation would be a purely military maneuver and believed its legitimacy after the war to be uncertain. His preferred long-term answer, and the answer his successor Johnson also would aim to follow, was the colonization of free slaves outside the United States. But first the Union would have to be "reconstructed," and both Lincoln and Johnson viewed as necessary a Thirteenth Amendment to the Constitution proscribing slavery.

Following the assassination of Lincoln, Johnson and the Republican Congress moved forward with reconstruction. Johnson wanted to resume civil government in the South as soon as possible, and to those in the states charged with carrying out his policy, he explained the conditions that would have to be met: repudiation of the Confederate debt; nullification of the ordinances of secession; and ratification of the Thirteenth Amendment abolishing slavery.[24] Mississippi refused to ratify the Amendment, but all other southern states did, and Johnson's effort to secure passage of the Amendment, Eric McKitrick observes, altogether went relatively smoothly.[25] Johnson's efforts earned him the praise or respect of several newspapers.[26] Johnson, in fact, even earned the praise of Democrats. "They were so overwhelmingly for him that it was almost embarrassing,"[27] and therein lies the source of a fundamental division between the Republican Congress and Johnson that would occur.

"The climax of reconstruction, in Johnson's mind," according to McKitrick, "appeared to be ratification of the Thirteenth Amendment."[28] Johnson was concerned about the "black codes" adopted by southern legislatures and hoped that southern states would extend the suffrage to

---

[24]Eric L. McKitrick, *Andrew Johnson and Reconstruction*, (New York: Oxford University Press, 1960), p. 161.

[25]*Id.*, p. 168.

[26]*Id.*, pp. 170-71.

[27]*Id.*, p. 172.

[28]*Id.*, p. 255.

Negroes, but he apparently did not believe it was within the purview of either his office or the national government to require any more of the southern states.[29]   All of the provisional governments in the south proceeded to restrict the suffrage to whites.   In Louisiana, a state Democratic convention declared that "we hold this to be a Government of White People, made and to be perpetuated for the exclusive political benefit of the White Race, and . . . that the people of African descent cannot be considered as citizens of the United States."[30] The black codes, according to Stampp, aimed to keep the Negro "a propertyless rural laborer under strict controls, without political rights, and with inferior legal rights."[31]

---

[29]Kenneth Stampp, *The Era of Reconstruction, 1865-1877*, p. 77.

[30]Quoted in Stampp, *id.*, p. 78.

[31]*Id.*, p. 79. Stampp summarizes the overall provisions of codes as follows:

Among their numerous provisions, the codes legalized Negro marriages, permitted Negroes to hold and dispose of property, to sue and be sued. They also took steps toward the establishment of racial segregation in public places. They prohibited inter-racial marriages, prohibited Negroes from serving on juries or testifying against white men, and re-enacted many of the criminal provisions of the prewar slave codes.   In the economic sphere, South Carolina prohibited Negroes from entering any employment except agricultural labor without special license; Mississippi would not permit them to buy or rent farm land; these states and others provided that Negroes found without lawful employment were to be arrested as vagrants and auctioned off or hired to landholders who would pay their fines. Louisiana required all Negro agricultural laborers to make contracts with landholders during the first ten days of January; once made, the contracts were binding for the year. Thereafter the Negroes were not permitted to leave their places of employment without permission. A Negro who refused to labor for his employer was to be arrested and put to forced labor on public works without compensation until he agreed to go back to his job.

Id., p. 80.

–*The Fourteenth Amendment*

In December of 1865, on the first day of the first session of Congress after Johnson assumed the Presidency, Congress formed a Joint Committee on Reconstruction for the purpose of assessing whether the former Confederate states were entitled to be represented in either house of Congress. Though engineered by the one of the "radical" Republicans, Representative Thaddeus Stevens, the measure passed, as McKitrick observes, "with great ease--without a fight, without amendments, and by a great majority. Stevens or no Stevens, most moderate Republicans thought it a perfectly proper and necessary thing."[32] The balance of power, in fact, lay with the moderate or more conservative Republicans. In January of 1866, Senator Lyman Trumbull introduced two bills, one the Freedman's Bureau Bill and the other a Civil Rights Bill. "The immediate stimulus for these measures," McKitrick observes, "had been the feeling that federal action of some sort was needed to halt the Southern legislatures in their work of Negro code-making."[33] The Freedman's Bureau Bill was designed to supplement the powers and extend the life of the Freedman's Bureau created during the last month of Lincoln's administration. As revised, the Bureau would be responsible for addressing problems faced by ex-slaves and refugees, both non-white and white, created by the rebellion, and its functions involved the establishment of schools, distribution of abandoned lands, and, in some cases, protect civil rights.[34] Trumbull's Civil Rights Bill "was an effort to give permanent, explicit, and general application to certain principles implied both in the Freedman's Bureau Bill and, presumably, in the Thirteenth Amendment."[35] The Civil Rights Bill conferred citizenship upon all persons born in the United States, save those subject to a foreign power and Indians not taxed, and it specified that the citizenship of such persons in the states and territories gives them the right to make and

---

[32]McKitrick, *Andrew Johnson and Reconstruction*, p. 259.

[33]*Id.*, p. 277.

[34]*Id.*, p. 278.

[35]*Id.*, p. 279.

enforce contracts, sue and be sued, freely hold and convey real and personal property, and to "full and equal benefit of all laws and proceedings for the security of person and property as is enjoyed by white citizens . . ."[36]

Congress eventually approved both bills, and Johnson vetoed both. Johnson vetoed the Freedman's Bureau Bill, claiming that it was unnecessary because the first Bureau measure had not expired, that it unconstitutionally expanded the peacetime power of the military, and that it was too expensive, to name just a few of his stated reasons. Johnson's veto message contained a passage particularly disturbing to the bill's supporters. Johnson suggested that no legislation concerning the southern states should be passed unless these same states were participants in the legislative process.[37] Johnson later commented that radical elements in Congress were leading another rebellion against the Constitution and that two of the radicals, Thaddeus Stevens and Charles Sumner, were conspiring to assassinate him.[38] The Republicans fell short of being able to override Johnson's veto of the Freedman's Bureau Bill.

Johnson vetoed the Civil Rights Bill, on the ground that such a policy could not be taken without the eleven of the states concerned first represented in Congress. He also thought the bill would enact "a perfect equality of the white and colored races" and therefore impose federal law in an area where it had "frequently been thought expedient to discriminate between the races."[39] Johnson also feared that if any of the rights protected in the Bill were denied in any state, federal courts would assume jurisdiction.[40] Congress overrode Johnson's veto and passed the Civil Rights Bill into law.

---

[36] *Id.*

[37] *Id.*, p. 289.

[38] *Id.*, pp. 292-93.

[39] *Id.*, p. 314.

[40] *Id.*

The re-passage of the Civil Rights Bill, as McKitrick observes, gave notice that the Senate would not accept the President's version of reconstruction. Congress' own version of reconstruction, one which attempted to address the consequences of emancipation, would be set out in a proposed Fourteenth Amendment to the Constitution.[41] The development of a Fourteenth Amendment was a protracted, six-month affair, but what seems most important about the process of reaching a final version of the Amendment is the compromise involved. Negro suffrage had been an objective of several Radical Republicans, such as Sumner, but political leaders in the Middle Atlantic and Midwest feared an express guarantee of Negro suffrage. Another divisive issue was that of Southern representation. Midwesterners tended to favor representation based on qualified voters. New Englanders opposed this plan, in consideration of their own dwindling representation.[42]

One other issue, which became particularly important in terms of long-term constitutional transformation, was whether the Fourteenth Amendment would be considered a temporary or a permanent settlement to the reconstruction question. Several radicals wanted the plan to be only temporary, in the hope that future majorities would seek more stern measures of reconstruction. "But the majority sentiment throughout the winter, spring, and summer of 1866 favored offering the South a clear settlement that could be accepted or rejected. The general feeling was for a re-establishment of the Union upon principles mutually recognized ..."[43]

After a series of negotiations and drafts, the Fourteenth Amendment reached what would be its final form in May of 1866.[44] A Negro suffrage

---

[41]*Id.*, p. 326.

[42]*Id.*, pp. 332-33.

[43]*Id.*, pp. 333.

[44]The Fourteenth Amendment reads:

Section 1. All persons born or naturalized in the United States, and subject to the jurisdiction thereof, are citizens of the United States and of the State wherein they reside. No State shall make or enforce any law which shall abridge the privileges or immunities of citizens of the United States; nor shall any State deprive any person of life, liberty, or property, without due process of law; nor deny to any person within its jurisdiction the equal protection of the laws.

Section 2. Representatives shall be apportioned among the several States according to their respective numbers, counting the whole number of persons in each State, excluding Indians not taxed. But when the right to vote at any election for the choice of electors for President and Vice President of the United States, Representatives in Congress, the Executive and Judicial officers of a State, or the members of the Legislature thereof, is denied to any of the male inhabitants of such State, being twenty-one years of age, and citizens of the United States, or in any way abridged, except for participation in rebellion, or other crime, the basis of representation therein shall be reduced in the proportion which the number of such male citizens shall bear to the whole number of male citizens twenty-one years of age in such State.

Section 3. No person shall be a Senator of Representative in Congress, or elector of President and Vice President, or hold any office, civil or military, under the United States, or under any State, who having previously taken an oath, as a member of Congress, or as an officer of the United States, or as a member of any State legislature, or as an executive or judicial officer of any State, to support the Constitution of the United States, shall have engaged in insurrection or rebellion against the same, or given aid or comfort to the enemies thereof. But Congress may by a vote of two-thirds of each House, remove such disability.

Section 4. The validity of the public debt of the United States, authorized by law, including debts incurred for payment of pensions and bounties for services in suppressing insurrection or rebellion, shall not be questioned. But neither the United States nor any State shall assume or pay any debt or obligation incurred in aid or insurrection or rebellion against the United States, or any claim for the loss of emancipation of any slave; but all such debts, obligations and claims shall be held illegal and void.

Section 5. The Congress shall have power to enforce, by appropriate provision had been struck from one of the last proposed plans.[45] What rights, then, were protected? No more, it would seem, than what Republican Representative James Wilson said when introducing the Civil Rights Bill of 1866. In his explanation of the "privileges or immunities" provision of the Bill, which the Fourteenth Amendment largely reproduces in its first section, Wilson comments:

> Do [the terms "privileges or immunities"] mean that in all things civil, social, political, all citizens without distinction of race or color, shall be equal? By no means can they be so construed. Do they mean that all citizens shall vote in the several states? No. . . . Nor do they mean that all citizens shall sit on the juries, or that their children shall attend the same schools. These are not civil rights or immunities. Well, what is the meaning? What are the civil rights? I understand civil rights to be simply the absolute rights of individuals, such as–"The right of personal security, the right of personal liberty, and the right to acquire and enjoy property."[46]

The Republican Party voted as a unit in favor of the final version of the Amendment. That it ultimately was a modest proposal, in comparison what several Radicals had wanted, is evidenced in its lack of overwhelming support from any particular groups, and the recognition by newspapers that plan was not far from what Johnson had wanted for reconstruction.[47]

---

legislation, the provisions of this article.

U.S. Const., Amend. 14.

[45]*Id.*, p. 347.

[46]As quoted in Paul Brest and Sanford Levinson, *Processes of Constitutional Decisionmaking: Cases and Materials*, 2nd ed., (Boston: Little, Brown & Co., 1983).

[47]McKitrick, *Andrew Johnson and Reconstruction*, pp. 355-56.

The Amendment, nevertheless, was unacceptable to Johnson as a term of reconstruction and to most southern states. Johnson pledged to vote for defeat of all Republican members of Congress who opposed his own reconstruction plan in the upcoming 1866 elections, and maintained that southern states should not have to ratify the Fourteenth Amendment before readmission to Congress. All of the southern states except Tennessee initially voted against the Fourteenth Amendment.

The chief issue in the 1866 congressional elections proved to be the immediate and unequivocal readmission of southern states to congressional representation,[48] although, as McKitrick observes, the tariffs and greenback currency could have been made issues.[49] Prior to the election, the National Union movement had emerged, calling for a great national organization committed to restoration of southern representation in Congress as soon as possible. But this pro-Johnson attempt at a third party eventually was subsumed by the Democratic Party. The partisan division in the 1866 elections thus is easy to organize: The Republicans required ratification of the Fourteenth Amendment by the former Confederate states before these states would regain congressional representation. The Democrats advocated immediate readmission of these southern states.

The Republicans won the elections triumphantly, and a case might be made that the whole reconstruction matter was settled at this point: By referendum, southern states would have to ratify the Fourteenth Amendment, and then reconstruction would be complete. Indeed, as McKitrick notes:

> A great majority of the Northern public and of Republican party leaders in the various states assumed that the Amendment was Congress' alternative to the Johnson policy and that it represented Congress' terms to the South.[50]

---

[48]*Id.*, p. 421.

[49]*Id.*, pp. 367-77.

[50]*Id.*, p. 449.

The elections, because they were so unequivocal, even generated feelings of satisfaction and relief; the great reconstruction question was now indisputably settled.[51] But not all Republicans viewed the Fourteenth Amendment as an exhaustive set of terms for southern readmission to Congress. This was, in fact, the reason that the matter had been left open when the Amendment was approved in Congress.[52] Since the agreement, several southern states had rejected the Amendment. Already the "radical" Republicans had agreed that the provisional state governments in the South, which had been set up by Johnson, must be replaced, temporarily, with direct federal rule. Following the 1866 elections, on the first day of the new session of Congress, a resolution to establish such governments was introduced.

–Negro Suffrage and the Fifteenth Amendment

The case for expanded congressional policy became stronger, McKitrick observes, as time went on. The governments set up by the President maintained their opposition to the Fourteenth Amendment, and accounts of persecution of both Unionists and Negroes in the south increasingly gained Northern attention. "A government with any claim to legitimacy, so went the argument, must at the least be able to maintain law and order."[53] Even after being warned that military reconstruction was not a bluff by the Republican Congress, Democrats refused to pass the Fourteenth Amendment. After overriding Johnson's veto, Congress passed the Military Reconstruction Acts in March of 1867, which required southern governments to enact Negro suffrage and to ratify the Fourteenth Amendment, and which required the supervisory presence of federal officials.

DID ANY OF THE TRANSFORMATIVE PROPOSALS HAVE WIDESPREAD SUPPORT BEYOND THE REALIGNING ERA?

---

[51]*Id.*, p. 450.

[52]*Id.*, p. 451, 361-62.

[53]*Id.*, p. 456.

1. Federal Authority to Restrict Slavery

A conservative president led a campaign to persuade the rebel states of the South to ratify the Thirteenth Amendment as one of the reconstructive terms, following the South's loss in a civil war waged largely over the question of federal authority to restrict slavery. Almost all of the rebel states quickly ratified the Amendment. The federal prohibition of slavery has not been challenged seriously in the United States since.

2. The Legitimacy of Secession

The question of whether a state has a legitimate right to secede from the Union predates the Civil War[54] and post-dates it, too. Lincoln's theory of the war, however, was the indissolubility of the Union. The Union victory could be said to have settled the matter for all practical purposes, and it probably does. But in his address at Gettysburg, as Gary Wills observes, Lincoln seems to suggest that the Declaration of Independence is the country's founding document, which is important because the Declaration was the "sovereign act of a single people."[55] The Constitution is a subsequent product of this same single people. This fact is why the Confederate states, and at least most of the soldiers fighting for them, on Lincoln's view of the Civil War, must be understood as rebels but not ex-patriots. A similar theory would be employed by the Supreme Court shortly after the Civil War. In 1869, in *Texas v. White*,[56] the U.S. Supreme Court ruled in favor of Texas's action for recovery of federal bonds it owned before secession. In order to have jurisdiction over the case, Texas would have to be a legitimate state, but the state, some years earlier, had claimed to have seceded from the Union. Chief

---

[54]*See* William Rawle, *A View of the Constitution of the United States of America*, 2nd ed., (New York: Da Capo Press, 1970, originally published in 1825), pp. 296-97.

[55]Gary Wills, *Lincoln at Gettysburg: The Words That Remade America*, (New York: Simon & Schuster, 1992), p. 132.

[56]74 U.S. (7 Wall.) 700 (1869).

Justice Samuel Chase, a Lincoln appointee, ruled secession unconstitutional, noting that the Articles of Confederation had declared the Union perpetual and the preamble to the 1789 Constitution declared the Union now to be even more perfect.[57]

3. Unilateral Military Power of the Executive

The Republican-controlled Congress retroactively ratified Lincoln's blockade and seizure of cargo from Confederate ships, his enlistment actions, and the suspension of habeas corpus. In *The Prize Cases*,[58] the Supreme Court reviewed the legitimacy of the blockade question and Congress's retroactive authorization of Lincoln's related measures. The dispositive matter, the Court reasoned, was that a state of war existed between April and July of 1861, so that the President had the authority to resist it in the manner taken. If it were necessary to have legislative approval of the President's actions, the Court also noted, then Congress's subsequent authorization would suffice. But, as Randall points out, the initial authorization measure passed by Congress was silent on the habeas corpus issue specifically, and Congress later struggled to reach an agreement regarding presidential suspension of habeas corpus. The agreement reached on March 3, 1863 approved presidential suspension of habeas corpus anytime during the rebellion that the President believed it appropriate, but it appears intentionally unclear whether Congress was "recognizing" the President's authority or granting it to him.[59] It also is interesting that passed with the Habeas Corpus Act was an Indemnity Act protecting federal officers from civil or criminal liability for carrying out orders of the President. Many supporters of the Indemnity Act, and probably more of its detractors, recognized that one major reason for passing the act was doubt about the legitimacy of presidential suspension of habeas corpus.[60]

---

[57] 74 U.S. (7 Wall.) at 724-35

[58] *The Prize Cases*, 67 U.S. 635 (1862).

[59] J.G. Randall, *Constitutional Problems Under Lincoln*, pp. 129-30.

[60] *See id.*, pp. 192-93.

The trial of civilians by military commissions did not fare as well as other executive uses of military authority. The Supreme Court in 1866 reviewed a death sentence case arising from a military commission in Indiana and ruled the military trial of a civilian unconstitutional, at least in cases in which civil authority may be substituted.[61]

4. National, Administrative Political Economy

It is not clear that during the 1860s or 1870s there ever was a national referendum on the Republican political economy implemented during the Civil War. McKitrick observes, the issues were there[62] to be exploited by Johnson in the 1866 congressional elections, but that attention focused squarely on the reconstruction questions–and the Democrats lost big. There eventually would be a national referendum on the matter two decades later, however, and the realignment pertaining to the industrial future of the country is the subject of the next chapter. That a referendum eventually would occur, of course, suggests that the Republican political economy measures survived, to some degree, over the course of the next two decades.

The banking system re-established by Congress in 1863, for example, would gain legitimacy. In 1869, in *Veazie Bank v. Fenno*,[63] the Supreme Court, according to Bray Hammond, "settled the Court back in the Hamiltonian channel from which the Jacksonians had deflected it."[64] The case involved the legitimacy of a federal prohibitive tax on state bank notes. Writing for the Court, Chief Justice Chase recognized that the tax could destroy state banks, but, he reasoned, Congress has

---

[61]*Ex parte Milligan*, 71 U.S. (4 Wall.) 2 (1866).

[62]*See* McKitrick, *Andrew Johnson and Reconstruction*.

[63]75 U.S. (8 Wall.) 533 (1869).

[64]Bray Hammond, *Banks and Politics in America From the Revolution to the Civil War*, (Princeton: Princeton University Press, 1957), p. 734.

exclusive power over the monetary system.[65]   But in 1870, it should be noted, the Court, with Chase again writing for the majority, struck down the Legal Tender Act of 1870, which had made greenbacks legal tender for the payment of debts.[66]   Perhaps the most interesting of Chase's arguments was that greenbacks were not necessary and proper to express congressional authority.[67]

The administrative capacities of the national government established with the Bank Act, the Department of Agriculture, and the subsidization of railroads also gained strength in subsequent decades. The 1870s, for example, witnessed a movement toward reform in the civil service system.   As Stephen Skowronek observes, "The reform of civil administration was, as its champions well knew, a logical response to the arrival of a new stage of national development."[68] The development of railroads encouraged by the national government eventually was greeted with a demand for national regulation of railroads. In 1886, the Supreme Court made national legislative action necessary by striking down a state law prohibiting railway long-haul rate discrimination as an intrusion on federal interstate commerce authority.[69] In light of the relatively unconsolidated features of central state development in the United States reaching back to its inception, this demand for regulation posed the challenge of "forging an entirely new mode of government operations at a time when the political and institutional arrangements underlying the established mode were being reinforced."[70] Though impeded by cross-

---

[65]*Veazie Bank v. Fenno*, 75 U.S. (8 Wall.) at 548.

[66]*Hepburn v. Griswold*, 75 U.S. (8 Wall.) 603 (1870).

[67]75 U.S. (8 Wall.) at 615-16.

[68]Stephen Skowronek, *Building a New American State: The Expansion of National Administrative Capacities, 1877-1920*, (Cambridge: Cambridge University Press, 1982), p. 49.

[69]*Wabash, St. Louis and Pacific Railway v. Illinois*, 118 U.S. 557 (1886).

[70]Skowronek, *Building a New American State*, p. 122.

cutting institutional arrangements, the first regulatory agency in the United States, the Interstate Commerce Commission, was established in 1887, for the purpose of insuring that all charges for rail transportation in interstate commerce would be reasonable and just. Unjust charges would be illegal, but the Commission possessed no authority to set rates. Agriculture, moreover, continued to benefit from governmental action, beyond the Department of Agriculture. "The land-grant and homesteading acts," as Theodore Lowi observes, "were followed by governmental services in research, quarantine, and education."[71]

5. Political and Social Equality of Black Men [72]

The legislative intent behind both the Fourteenth and Fifteenth Amendments has been established in this study of the development of these Amendments, and other studies have reached similar findings.[73] The long-term meaning of the Amendments is less clear, however, once the partisan politics of the Civil War and Reconstruction stabilize in the 1870s. When military reconstruction ends, the Amendments seem informally rewritten to accommodate an interest in stability.

The Radical Republicans successfully implemented military

---

[71]Theodore Lowi, *The End of Liberalism: The Second Republic of the United States*, 2nd ed., (New York: W.W. Norton, 1979), p. 70.

[72]Women were not intended to be the beneficiary of an expanded right of suffrage in the 1860s and 1870s. For that reason, the early women's movement opposed ratification of the Fifteenth Amendment, which, by its terms, did not prohibit suffrage discrimination on the basis of gender. The Nineteenth Amendment, ratified in 1920, guarantees woman suffrage.

[73]Most notably: Raoul Berger, *Government By Judiciary: The Transformation of the Fourteenth Amendment*, (Cambridge: Harvard University Press, 1977), and Alexander M. Bickel, "The Original Understanding and the Segregation Decision," 69 *Harvard Law Review* 1 (1955). Expansive interpretations of the Amendment include: Horace E. Flack, *The Adoption of the Fourteenth Amendment*, (Baltimore: Johns Hopkins University Press, 1908), and Jacobus tenBroek, *The Antislavery Origins of the Fourteenth Amendment* (Berkeley: University of California Press, 1951).

reconstruction and secured ratification of the Fifteenth Amendment, which guaranteed Negro suffrage. But Radical Reconstruction, for all its gains, resulted in a political backlash in the South and may have proved too cumbersome for a significant number of Republicans. The Radical governments in the South helped to establish schools, poverty relief, and institutions for the disadvantaged, and they helped to repair or rebuild public roads, bridges, and buildings. Corruption and abuse also occurred under these regimes, but as Tindall notes, corruption occurred both before and after Reconstruction, and among both Republicans and Democrats.[74] Probably more problematic for the Republican regimes was the terrorism levied against "carpetbaggers" and blacks by the Ku Klux Klan. Congress attempted to help by passing three Enforcement Acts between 1870 and 1871, including a Ku Klux Klan Act of 1871. These acts outlawed the interference with anyone's right to vote and placed congressional elections under surveillance by federal election supervisors. The Ku Klux Klan Act outlawed characteristic activities of the Klan, such as conspiracies and intimidation.[75]

Ironically, this attempt to bolster the Reconstruction regimes engendered important criticism among some Republicans. Lyman Trumbull insisted that the states must remain "the depositories of the rights of the individual."[76] If Congress could enact a criminal code and thereby define and punished offenses as traditionally done by states, "what is the need of the State governments?"[77] The abolitionist Carl Schurz considered the Ku Klux Klan Act unconstitutional. A major breach among Republicans over Reconstruction did not occur at this time, but this criticism did set the stage for a foretelling Liberal Republican movement of 1872.

By the close of Ulysses Grant's administration, calls for reform of the

---

[74]Tindall, *America: A Narrative History*, vol. 1, p. 692.

[75]*See id.*, p. 694.

[76]Quoted in Eric Foner, *Reconstruction*, p. 456.

[77]Quoted in Foner, *id.*

Republican Party had mounted, grounded in charges that the party was controlled by party machines and mired in patronage battles. Classical liberalism, which had been the major premise of Jacksonian ideology, had emerged as a prospective "science" for reform within the new consolidated American state, which could be understood and utilized by "experts." The ideology helped experts to distinguish between legislation enacted for the common good and that which actually was "class legislation."[78] The ideology, as Foner observes, also was used to support Carl Schurz's contention that the Deep South could never evolve into stable republican government, so that further federal intervention would be pointless.[79] Yet an increasing disenchantment with Reconstruction, Foner explains, was from a variety of sources, not just liberal ideology:

> Many saw the Southern question as an annoying distraction that enabled party spoilsmen to retain the allegiance of voters by waving the bloody shirt, while preventing tariff reduction, civil service reform, and good government from taking the center stage of politics. Although they had supported, indeed helped to formulate, the Reconstruction Acts and postwar amendments, reformers insisted more strenuously than other Republicans that with the principle of equal rights secured, the party should move on to the "living issues."[80]

Before the 1872 election, Republican reformers moved to organize a new party premised on civil service reform, tariff reduction, lower taxes, an end to land grants to railroads, and the resumption of specie payments.[81] These Liberals called for a convention to nominate a presidential candidate, who would be Horace Greely. Grant won the election, but the significant support for Greely "demonstrated once for all the death of

---

[78]*See* Foner, *Reconstruction*, pp. 488-93.

[79]*Id.*, p. 497.

[80]*Id.*, p. 497.

[81]*Id.*, p. 500.

Radicalism as both a political movement and a coherent ideology."[82] The economic downturn beginning the next year must have underscored the point. In 1873, the country would experience its first great crisis of industrial capitalism, an economic depression, triggered apparently by overexpansion of the railroad network financed by speculative credit. "By the end of 1874, nearly half the nation's iron furnaces had suspended operation. Not until 1878, a year that saw more than 10,000 business fail, did the depression reach bottom."[83]

The official reversal of Radical Reconstruction came in the Compromise of 1876. The presidential election between the Republican Rutherford Hayes and the Democrat Samuel Tilden proved enormously contestable. Tilden won the popular vote, but Hayes won the electoral votes by a margin of one. As Foner reports, a crisis emerged:

> Predictably, Republican election boards in Florida, South Carolina, and Louisiana invalidated enough returns from counties rife with violence to declare Hayes and the party's candidate for governor victorious. Equally predictably, Democrats challenged the results. Rival state governments assembled in Louisiana and South Carolina, and rival election certificates were dispatched to Washington.[84]

The crisis would be resolved by an agreement between the Republicans and Democrats. The Democrats would not contest the outcome, if the Republicans agreed to end Reconstruction. The precise specifics of the agreement, Foner explains, are not easily determinable,[85] but Hayes became President and "1877 marked a decisive retreat from the idea, born during the Civil War, of a powerful nation protecting the

---

[82]*Id.*, p. 510.

[83]*Id.* p. 512.

[84]*Id.*, pp. 575-76.

[85]*Id.*, p. 581.

fundamental rights of American citizens."[86]

Marginal support for Reconstruction by the 1870s and an eventual abandonment of strong protection of the fundamental rights of blacks also are evidenced in Supreme Court decisions regarding the Civil War Amendments. In its first opportunity to interpret the Fourteenth Amendment, the *Slaughterhouse Cases*[87] of 1871, the Supreme Court violates the text and historical meaning of the Amendment by dividing citizenship into national and state categories and reasoning that the citizenship protected by the Amendment is only national citizenship. The privileges and immunities attached to national citizenship turn out not to be the ones contemplated by the legislative intent of the Amendment, i.e., the right to own property, freely convey it, and enter into and enforce contracts; these are the privileges of *state* citizenship. *National* citizenship, Justice Miller explains, consists of a relatively few rights arising from a person's relationship to the national government, such as the right to petition the national government, to engage in interstate commerce, and to be protected by the national government while in another country.[88] In other cases, however, the Supreme Court and state courts correctly recognized that the Privileges or Immunities Clause is implicated by questions of the legitimacy of racial distinctions in the distribution of opportunities, but they held that racial distinctions were legitimate under the Clause.[89]

---

[86]*Id.*, p. 582.

[87]83 U.S. 36 (1872).

[88]*See* 83 U.S. at 75-80.

[89]*E.g., In re Hobbs*, 1 U.S. (Woods) 537 (1871) (sustaining a state miscegenation statute); *Cory v. Cater*, 48 Ind. 344 (1874) (sustaining separate schools for children of different races); *Ohio Valley Railway v. Lander*, 104 Ky. 431 (1898) (sustaining a statute requiring separate seating of passengers on a coach).

In 1883, in the *Civil Rights Cases*,[90] the Supreme Court retrenches congressional legislation protecting civil rights passed just before the end of Reconstruction. The Civil Rights Act of 1875 had guaranteed to all persons in the United States the equal enjoyment of places of public accommodations, facilities, inns, conveyances on land or water, and places of amusement. The Court finds the Act unconstitutional. Writing for the Court, Justice Joseph Bradley explains that the text of the Fourteenth Amendment proscribes only on *state* actions that violate civil rights, not the actions of individuals.   Violations of civil rights by individuals alone, without state authority, may be redressed only through state law.   The Thirteenth Amendment, Bradley continues, simply proscribes slavery and is not implicated by the discriminatory actions of individuals. He observes:

> It would be running the slavery argument into the ground to make it apply to every act of discrimination which a person may see fit to make as to the guests he will entertain, or as to the people he will take into his coach or cab or car, or admit to his concert or theatre, or deal with in other matters of intercourse or business.[91]

This quashing of Congress's last Reconstruction effort to protect the fundamental rights of blacks seems to resurrect the original legislative intent behind the Fourteenth Amendment, which is modest in scope and allowed for a variety of social distinctions between blacks and whites to be made under the color of law.[92] It seems to authorize the segregation

---

[90] 109 U.S. 3 (1883).

[91] 109 U.S. at 24-25.

[92] The "original intent" established in this research is not a new finding. In the law clerk's letter conveying a research memorandum to Supreme Court Justice Felix Frankfurter, Alexander Bickel comments:

> It was preposterous [during passage of the Fourteenth Amendment] to worry about unsegregated schools, for example, when hardly a beginning had been made at educating Negroes at all and when obviously special efforts, suitable only for Negroes, would have to be

and, at least to a degree, the black codes that had developed just after the Civil War and that were the targets of Radical Republicans. The classic argument against moving beyond the political equality of blacks toward social equality was made by Andrew Johnson in his third annual message to Congress. Johnson acknowledged that blacks were entitled to humane treatment by government, but:

> it must be acknowledged that in the progress of nations negroes have shown less capacity for government than any other race of people. No independent government of any form has ever been successful in their hands. On the contrary, wherever they have been left to their own devices they have shown a constant tendency to relapse into barbarism. . . . Of all the dangers which our nation has yet encountered, none are equal to those which must result from the success of the effort now making to Africanize the [southern] half of our country.[93]

In 1896, in *Plessy v. Ferguson*,[94] the Supreme Court echoed Johnson's analysis in affirming the apartheid that had been established in the South. Writing for the Court, Justice Henry Brown reasons:

> If the two races are to meet upon terms of social equality, it must be the result of natural affinities, a mutual appreciation of each other's merits and a voluntary consent of individuals. . . . Legislation is powerless to eradicate racial instincts or to abolish distinctions based upon physical differences, and the attempt to do so can only result in accentuating the difficulties of the present situation. If the civil and political rights of both races

---

made . . . In any event, it is impossible to conclude that the 39th Congress intended segregation be abolished; impossible to conclude that they foresaw it might be, under the language they were adopting.

Reported in Richard Kluger, *Simple Justice*, (New York: Vintage, 1975), p. 654.

[93]Quoted in Kenneth Stampp, *The Era of Reconstruction*, p. 87.

[94]163 U.S. 537 (1896).

be equal one cannot be inferior to the other civilly or politically. If one race be inferior to the other socially, the Constitution of the United States cannot put them on the same plane. . . .[95]

CONCLUSIONS

The series of fundamental changes described above may well mark what Bruce Ackerman terms the beginning of the second American constitutional "regime."[96]

---

[95] 163 U.S. at 551-52.

[96] Ackerman, *We the People: Foundations* (Cambridge: Harvard University Press, 1991), chs. 3-4.

5. THE 1890s REFERENDUM ON FEDERAL PROTECTION OF THE ECONOMY

In the 1890s, about twenty years after the critical realignment begun in the 1850s finally stabilized, another partisan realignment would occur. Since the 1860s, the Republican Party had managed to retain governmental dominance, though the two-party system had been extremely competitive since 1876.[1] But by the late 1870s, both major parties were pursuing pro-industrial policies. It was in the 1890s that agricultural interests managed to set the agenda within the Democratic Party, following the economic crisis of 1893, and led the Party to challenge the pro-industry principles of the Republicans. In the 1894 congressional elections, however, the Democrats lost a record 113 seats in Congress. In the presidential election of 1896, the Democratic candidate William Jennings Bryan led a fiery oratorical campaign against the Republicans, represented by William McKinley, but Bryan lost the election. Most importantly, transformative policy change rooted in the specific issues driving the 1890s realignment did not follow. The long-standing status quo won. The elections resulted in the consolidation of Republican Party strength, not in the upheaval of Republican policies. It thus might seem that this "realignment" either was not actually a realignment at all or was of one a qualitatively different sort. We also

---

[1]But, as Walter Dean Burnham notes, "During the twenty-two years from 1875 to 1897, a single party controlled [the White House, the Senate, and the House of Representatives] at the same time for only six years . . . . The truth was that during the second half of the Civil War system, there was no majority party; or rather, there were two majority parties, depending on where the focus of analysis lay. Such a condition was optimal for producing policy deadlocks at the center." Walter Dean Burnham, "The 1896 System: An Analysis," in Paul Kleppner, et al., *The Evolution of American Electoral Systems*, (Westport: Greenwood Press, 1981), p. 151.

would not expect to see informal constitutional change following these elections, one might suggest, because the status quo effectively prevailed.

Perhaps so, but American constitutional development and the contemporary constitutional order can be better understood with some attention paid to the national elections of the mid-1890s, precisely because the Democrats made these elections referenda on equivocal political economy commitments rooted in Republican initiatives of the 1860s. It must be remembered that Republican advancements of administrative techniques responsive to industrial interests in the early 1860s went unchallenged in Congress, perhaps because secession and the terms of Reconstruction were the central issues in the national elections of the late 1860s. In this chapter, the same test for transformative policy proposals and widespread support of them applied in the previous chapters will be applied to the 1890s realignment era. Given the results of these elections, of course, one might expect not to find major departures from the constitutional terrain of the past. But it may be that the elections served to consolidate and strengthen prior constitutional developments.

AT THE OUTSET OF THE 1890S REALIGNMENT, WAS CONSTITUTIONALLY TRANSFORMATIVE POLICY PROPOSED?

The Constitutional Status Quo Ante

In terms of political economy, those of the Jacksonian "persuasion" embraced "classical liberalism." The classical liberals, for the sake of clarity, had prescribed virtual free market economics. John Locke, for example, maintained that God gave the Earth to mankind for his expropriation and advanced a labor theory of property as justification for private property secure from governmental takings.[2] Adam Smith reasoned that individuals know better than government how best to employ capital, that there were more examples of successful private market undertakings than of unsuccessful ones, and that an individual's

---

[2]John Locke, *The Second Treatise on Civil Government*, (New York: Prometheus Books, 1986), p. 22.

pursuit of his own self-interest in the market would serve to help all of society, given the productive and efficient investments that would be made along the way. Jackson basically was successful in removing the federal government from an active role in protecting industries or sponsoring particular economic activity, although states became battlegrounds for government-granted privileges, and federal respect for the integrity of state internal affairs under Jacksonian political theory seems to have offered little counterweight to this development. Dominating Congress during the Civil War, Republicans established a national banking system, implemented the Homestead Act and land grants, increased protective tariffs, and renewed federal sponsorship of internal improvements, including railways, all of which served to encourage private economic development, but through government facilitation, not an unfettered market. To cope with the development, the Republicans also had established rudimentary administrative structures.

Over the course of the next two decades, both major parties in the United States pursued pro-industrial policies at the federal and state levels, despite the financial panic that over-production of goods and raw materials, over-capitalization of railroads, and speculation in securities brought in 1873.[3] "The underlying transformation between the Civil War and the turn of the century," Walter Dean Burnham reports," was the creation of an integrated industrial-capitalist political economy."[4] And "[f]rom its imperatives," he adds, "flowed the rapid influx of immigrants, urbanization and its manifold problems of social policy . . ."[5] While these developments entailed a number of sources of discontent, Burnham observes that among party elites, "there was no clear incentive for adapting programs and campaigns to new issues or for incorporating new dissenting groups into the already complex game of coalition

---

[3]For classic authority on these items as the cause of the Panic of 1873, *see* Samuel Eliot Morison, *The Oxford History of the American People: Volume Three, 1869-1963*, (New York: Penguin, 1972).

[4]*Id.*, p. 152.

[5]*Id.* See also Robert H. Wiebe, *The Search for Order 1877-1920*, (New York: Hill and Wang, 1967).

management."[6]

But the federal government did respond to select calls for regulation and reform. Civil Service reform and expanded regulatory activity emerged as means improving public administration and stabilizing competition within industries, respectively, and both were supported by businesses.[7] The U.S. Supreme Court, however, authorized some regulatory activity unfavorable to industrial interests. In 1877, in *Munn v. Illinois*[8], the Supreme Court upheld Granger-supported regulation aimed at preventing storage price abuses by a monopoly of grain elevator operators. The Court found that private property directed to a public use was subject to public regulation, pursuant to the police powers of a state for the protection of its citizens.[9] But the regulation upheld in *Munn* and the related Granger cases[10] was *intrastate* regulation. As Alfred Kelly, Winfred Harbison, and Herman Belz astutely observe, "At the same time that the Supreme Court sanctioned intrastate economic regulation, it took steps to bring an increasingly integrated national market under the protection of federal authority."[11] The dominant constitutional provision for integrating the national market was the interstate commerce clause, which generally was construed, in the period from 1873 to 1890, to

---

[6]*Id.*, p. 151; *see also* David W. Brady, *Critical Elections andCongressional Policy Making*, (Stanford: Stanford University Press, 1988), p. 51.

[7]*See* Stephen Skowronek, *Building a New American State: The Expansion of National Administrative Capacities, 1877-1920*, (Cambridge: Cambridge University Press, 1982), chs. 5 and 8.

[8]94 U.S. 113 (1877).

[9]94 U.S. at 126.

[10]The accompanying cases involved local and interstate railroads and were *Chicago, B. & Q. R. R. v. Iowa*, 94 U.S. 155 (1877) and *Peik v. Chicago & Nw. Ry.*, 94 U.S. 164 (1877).

[11]Alfred H. Kelly, Winfred A. Harbison, and Herman Belz, *The American Constitution*, p. 402.

preclude state regulation.

In *Welton v. Missouri*[12], for example, the Supreme Court declared a Missouri license tax on persons selling goods manufactured out of state unconstitutional, on the ground that federal commerce power protected articles of commerce until they ceased to be the subject of discrimination based on their foreign origin.[13] The decision served to "[protect] new marketing techniques that depended on direct dealing between manufacturers and local retailers."[14] Subsequent state license fees on sales agents representing out-of-state manufacturers without a regularly licensed local business also were found by the Supreme Court to be burdens on interstate commerce.[15] Even state inspection laws "when used to exclude out-of state shipments of meat prepared by the new national packing companies . . . were also declared unconstitutional."[16]

In terms of jurisprudence, most illustrative of increased protection of the national market was the Supreme Court's decision in a case concerning national transportation and communication facilities. In *Pensacola Telegraph Company v. Western Union Telegraph Company*[17], decided in 1877, Pensacola Company claimed the exclusive right to operate a telegraph business in the northern part of Florida, pursuant to state-granted privileges, while Western Union claimed the right to operate pursuant to an act of Congress, passed in 1866, allowing any company the right to construct telegraph lines in any part of the public domain of the U.S., subject to particular conditions. The Court found that the congressional act prohibited all state monopolies in this field of

---

[12]91 U.S. 275 (1875).

[13]91 U.S. at 282.

[14]Kelly, Harbison, and Belz, *The American Constitution*, p. 403.

[15]*Robbins v. Shelby County*, 120 U.S. 489 (1887).

[16]Kelly, Harbison, and Belz, *The American Constitution*, p. 403 (referring to *Minnesota v. Barber*, 136 U.S. 313 (1890)).

[17]96 U.S. 1 (1877).

interstate commerce.[18]

An expanded sense of federal commerce clause power also served to authorize the first federal regulatory agency in the United States, the Interstate Commerce Commission, in 1887. The Act creating the Commission was, as Theodore Lowi observes, classic administrative legislation. ". . . Congress (1) delegated its own power to regulate an aspect of interstate commerce (2) to an administrative agency (3) designed especially for the purpose."[19] Additional federal regulation of market activities emerged in 1890 with the passage of the Sherman Anti-Trust Act, and gradually would increase into the early twentieth century.[20]

Amid the integration of the national market, there also was one consistent fiscal policy in the post-Civil War decades–currency deflation. Following the inflation that had been caused by the War and issuance of "greenbacks", the deflation policy involved the retirement of Greenbacks and resumption of specie payments. But as Burnham observes, this fiscal policy actually spurred the development of resistance politics, which would lie at the roots of the major challenge in the 1890s to many of the post-War developments in political economy. The deflation, Burnham explains, coupled with the effects of the economic depression that had begun in 1873, produced a series of "political explosions," particularly the Greenbackers' uprising, which would foreshadow the volatile political realignment of 1894-96.

In this movement we see for the first time--almost in embryo–the basic strategy of those who were suffering from the

---

[18]96 U.S. 11 (1877).

[19]Theodore J. Lowi, *The End of Liberalism: The Second Republic of the United States*, 2nd ed. (New York: Norton, 1979), p. 95.

[20]Lowi notes, in fact, that as public controls evolved in the United States from 1887 forward, increased abstraction in what is to be regulated occurs, e.g., from concrete objects to categories of objsect, to qualities of things, to structures of relationships, to overall environments of conduct. *Id.*, pp. 98-99.

ascendancy of industrial capitalism: *the welding together of a* farmer-labor coalition devoted to a *political* overthrow of the "immutable economic laws" of laissez-faire capitalism [emphasis in original].[21]

It is not clear, however, that Burnham's use of the term "laissez faire" accurately captures the political-economic ideology that had become characteristic of federal and state government policy, for the term suggests that government did not favor any particular market outcomes. But the federal government had come to favor particular market outcomes–those favoring industrial-business interests–and so had some states. By the late 1880s, the new justices on the Supreme Court, by virtue of their social background and experience, were "sympathetic to the needs of railroads, corporations, and the entrepreneurial class in general."[22] Whereas earlier state police powers reliably were understood to allow for state regulation of business activity, beginning in the late 1880s, they less often survived judicial scrutiny, even at the state level. In *In re Jacobs*[23], for example, the New York Court of Appeals struck down a New York law restricting the manufacture of cigars in tenement houses. The law had been passed as a public health measure, but the Court of Appeals ruled that it arbitrarily deprived a cigar maker of liberty

---

[21]Burnham, "The 1896 System: An Analysis," p. 154.

[22]Kelly, Harbison, and Belz, *The American Constitution*, p. 404.

[23]98 N.Y. 98 (1885).

and property.[24]   In *Mugler v. Kansas*[25] the U.S. Supreme Court announced that claimed exercises of state police power would not automatically be accepted at face value. Justice John Marshall Harlan's majority opinion is particularly notable, in light of constitutional development in the twentieth century. The courts, he reasoned, are under a duty "to look at the substance of things, whenever they enter upon the inquiry whether the legislature has transcended the limits of authority."[26] If a law were to have no real relationship to the purported protection of health, welfare, or safety of the community and instead infringed on fundamental rights, it would be unconstitutional.[27] In 1890, in *Chicago, Milwaukee, and St. Paul Railway Co. v. Minnesota*[28], the Supreme Court claimed the authority, on procedural grounds, to review the reasonableness of a public utility rate regulation. In his dissent, Justice Bradley noted that this decision actually seemed to overrule *Munn v. Illinois*, because in the latter case rates were understood to be subject to public regulation, but now they were suggested to be *judicial* questions.[29]

---

[24]89 N.Y. at 132. In its majority opinion, in fact, the court reasons that:

> If [the legislature] passes an act ostensibly for the public health, and thereby destroys or takes away the property of a citizen or interferes with his personal liberty, then it is for the courts to scrutinize the act and see whether it really relates to and is convenient and appropriate to promote the public health.

Id.

[25]123 U.S. 623 (1887).

[26]123 U.S. at 661.

[27]*Ibid.*

[28]134 U.S. 418 (1890).

[29]134 U.S. at 462-64 ("By the decision now made we declare, in effect, that the judiciary, and not the legislature, is the final arbiter in the regulation of fares and freights of railroads and the charges of other public accommodations", at p. 463-64).

The momentum toward a pro-industry, federally-protected economy was derailed, however, by the Panic of 1893. "The economic crisis of 1893," realignment scholar David Brady argues, "crystallized opposition to the industrial revolution and led directly to the critical period of the 1890's (1894-96)."[30] Walter Dean Burnham comments that the "sudden, sharp blow of the 1890s was the catastrophic collapse of the economy in and after the spring of 1893."[31] The crisis allowed the "prosilver inflationists", to use Brady's term, to leverage influence within the Democratic Party and challenge industrial agenda of the Republican Party.[32]

Transformative Issues:

1. Currency/Specie

By 1895, the prosilver inflationists had gained control of the Democratic Party and sought coinage of silver at sixteen-to-one parity with gold. Many Democrats traditionally had been advocates of the gold standard, with President Grover Cleveland having firmly defended it. But the 1896 Democratic Party platform cites the currency issue as the paramount electoral issue, linking it to the contemporary economic crisis.

> Recognizing that the money question is paramount to all others at this time, we invite attention to the fact that the Federal Constitution named silver and gold together as the money metals of the United States. . . . We declare that the act of 1875 demonetizing silver without the knowledge or approval of the American people has resulted in the appreciation of gold and a corresponding fall in the prices of commodities produced by the people; a heavy increase in the burdens of taxation and of all

---

[30]David Brady, *Critical Elections and Congressional Policy Making*, (Stanford: Stanford University Press, 1988), p. 52.

[31]Burnham, "The 1896 System: An Analysis," p. 158.

[32]Lawrence Goodwyn's *The Populist Moment: A Short History of the Agrarian Revolt in America*, (Oxford: Oxford University Press, 1978) is an excellent accounting of the agrarian revolt and Populism.

debts, public and private; the enrichment of the money-lending class at home and abroad; the prostration of industry and impoverishment of the people.[33]

In 1879, the Republicans had implemented the policy of resuming specie payments. The Republican platform of 1896, as Brady reports, opposed the free coinage of silver, except by international agreement with the leading commercial nations of the earth.[34] The Republicans viewed "the free coinage of silver as a radical attempt to stifle free enterprise."[35]

2. Protective Tariffs

At the time of the party conventions of 1896, the tariff in place was the Democratic tariff implemented by President Cleveland. The Party advocated tariffs for the purpose of revenue, and that would operate equally across the nation, not discriminating between class or section; and the Party opposed any further changes in tariff laws. In term of the political-economic order, the Party also charged that the protective tariffs of the Republicans had bred trusts and monopolies, which, in turn, "enriched the few at the expense of the many, restricted trade, and deprived the producers of the great American staples of access to their natural markets."[36]

The Republicans advocated a return to the protective tariff of the Harrison Administration a few years earlier, citing protection as "the bulwark of American industrial independence, and the foundation of American development and prosperity."[37] The protective tariff, it was

---

[33]Quoted in Brady, *Critical Elections and Congressional Policy Making*, p. 54.

[34]Brady, p. 54.

[35]*Id.*, p. 54.

[36]Quoted in Brady, p. 55.

[37]*Id.*

argued, "led to an American market for American producers, the upholding of the American workingman's wages, equity between business and farming, and a diffusion of general thrift . . ."[38]

3. American Expansionism

American expansionism should be acknowledged as an electoral issue in 1894-96, yet it is not clear that it was a transformative one. As Brady notes, neither party questioned the legitimacy of American intervention in Latin America pursuant to the Monroe Doctrine. In their 1896 platform, the Republicans favored a Nicaraguan canal, the annexation of Hawaii, the purchase of Spanish islands, and the improvement of the U.S. Navy, while the Democrats, at their convention, did not deal with these particular extra-territorial issues. Instead, they advocated the placing of Alaskan forests and industries under U.S. laws. In regard to Cuba, the Republicans advocated the active use of American influence to restore peace in Cuba and to leverage its independence. The Democrats simply extended their sympathy to the people of Cuba, in regard to the latter's struggle for liberty and independence.[39] These were important differences in priorities but not differences regarding the principle of American expansionism or the legitimacy of American expansionism to date.

DID ANY CONSTITUTIONALLY TRANSFORMATIVE PROPOSAL HAVE WIDESPREAD SUPPORT BEYOND THE REALIGNING ERA?

Transformation rejected

In this case, the changes to the constitutional landscape advocated by the Democrats in the 1890s lost resoundingly at the polls. In 1894, the Democrats lost 113 seats in Congress. In 1896, the Republican McKinley comfortably won the presidential election over the Democrat Bryan. The realignment here thus did not prove "critical," with respect to public policy. As Richard McCormick explains, "critical realignment" seems

---

[38] *Id.*

[39] *Id.*

an inappropriate term to ascribe to this electoral upheaval, in consideration of how the transformative policy proposals were processed:

> If William Jennings Bryan had defeated William McKinley in 1896, significant changes might have followed. But Bryan lost, and for approximately another decade, until after the passage of the regulatory measures of 1906, national policies remained little altered. What is more, the specific policy disputes of the realigning years, currency and tariff, soon abated and scarcely shaped the major clashes over governance during the succeeding era (although the tariff issue flashed again into prominence around 1909). The main economic policy question of the decade after 1896 involved the search for a new and more satisfactory balance between the promotion and regulation of industry by government. This issue had barely been raised in 1896. And when it later did come to the fore it was not in any clear way a Democratic-versus-Republican question.[40]

Consolidation of the Status Quo: Increased Federal Authority to Protect the National Economy

Following the 1894-96 elections, Republicans were a dominant party and easily able to continue the policy directions they had pursued before these election. (See Table 5.1) They re-enacted the protective tariff and a passed a law securing gold as the monetary standard. And perhaps because the political economy leanings of the status quo were affirmed in these elections, there was no interruption in the political economy trends that had developed in the American polity before and through the 1890s. The nature of these elections and outcomes, in fact, provides useful hermeneutical context for contemporary and subsequent Supreme Court decisions.

---

[40]Richard L. McCormick, *The Party Period in Public Policy: American Politics from the Age of Jackson to the Progressive Era*, (New York: Oxford University Press, 1986).

TABLE 5.1[41]

Year	Congress	House Seats Reps. Dems.	Senate Seats Reps. Dems.
1891-93	52nd	88 235	47 39
1893-95	53rd	127 218	38 44
1895-97	54th	244 105	43 39
1897-99	55th	204 113	47 34
1899-1901	56th	185 163	53 26
1901-03	57th	197 151	55 31
1903-05	58th	208 178	57 33
1905-07	59th	250 136	57 33
1907-09	60th	222 164	61 31

The Supreme Court's decisions in *Field v. Clark*[42] and in *In re Debs*[43], for example, seem to have a more unequivocally legitimate basis, in consideration of consolidation of Republican party strength. In *Field v. Clark*, decided in 1892, the Supreme Court reviewed the Tariff Act of 1890's authorization of the President to stop the free importation of particular goods, if he were to find that the exporting country had imposed unequal and unreasonable duties on U.S. products. At issue was whether Congress could delegate its authority under Article I of the Constitution over this trade matter to the President–a separation of powers question. Writing for the majority, Justice John Marshall Harlan dismantled the question by reasoning that there had been no delegation, on the ground that Congress had designed the tariff policy, including the decision that tariffs should be placed on countries charging unreasonable duties on U.S. products. The President was charged only with carrying

---

[41]Adapted from: U. S. Bureau of the Census, *Historical Statistics of the United States, Colonial Times to 1957*, (Washington, 1960).

[42]143 U.S. 649 (1892).

[43]158 U.S. 564 (1895).

out a fact-finding mission, pursuant to the execution of the tariff law. David Currie finds this "ministerial" characterization of the President's responsibility under the act unconvincing,[44] but the decision has the effect of expanding federal protection of the economy, which is consonant with direction public policy had been heading. In *In re Debs*, the Court upheld the power of a federal court, pursuant to an executive order, to enjoin the interference with railway traffic during the Pullman strike of 1894. As Currie observes, what deserves most attention in the majority opinion in the case is that Justice David J. Brewer fails to identify the precise source of legal authority on which the injunction is based. Presidents only enforce the laws, and "Brewer nowhere argued that Congress had prohibited private obstructions to interstate rail traffic."[45] The effect of this decision, nevertheless, also was to expand federal protection of the economy.

In effect, the Court in these two cases expanded federal authority to integrate and to protect the national economy. Before the 1890s realignment, it is difficult to find much of a popular consensus for the federal authority over the economy it had assumed, since the roots of such expanded authority lay in Republican legislative successes absent southern delegations to Congress during the Civil War.[46] The 1894-96 realignment seems to suggest some consensus favoring this authority.

Federal integration of the market, however, would not mean that the federal government could intervene in the market willy nilly. In fact, the 1890s and early 1900s witnessed examples of limitations on federal authority to intervene in market affairs imposed by the Supreme Court, in addition to the previously more common limits on state intervention, and of Supreme Court deference to state and federal protective interventions into the economy. In *Pollock v. Farmers' Loan & Trust*

---

[44]David P. Currie, *The Constitution in the Supreme Court: The Second Century, 1888-1986*, (Chicago: University of Chicago Press, 1990), p. 18.

[45]*Id.*, p. 20.

[46]*See, supra*, Chapter Four.

Co.[47], for example, decided in 1895, the Supreme Court declared the federal income tax unconstitutional. The stated legal rationale for the decision was that the tax was not apportioned among the states by population, in violation of article I of the Constitution. But, as Currie suggests, this reasoning seems disingenuous, in consideration of previous decisions:

> This conclusion must have caused great surprise. Not only had the Justices repeatedly suggested in dicta that only capitation and land taxes were "direct"; twice in the preceding twenty-five years they had upheld income taxes, most recently on that precise ground. The dicta were dismissed as such in *Pollock*. The holdings were distinguished because one case had involved an excise tax calculated according to income and the other a taxpayer whose income was derived essentially from professional earnings rather than property, though neither of these facts had been offered as bases for the original decisions.[footnotes omitted][48]

In *United States v. E. C. Knight Co.*[49], also decided in 1895, the Supreme Court distinguished between manufacturing and commerce to strike down the application of the Sherman Anti-Trust Act to sugar acquisitions that had given one manufacturer ninety-eight percent of the sugar market. The dissent noted that the manufacturing monopoly at issue had the effect of infringing on the buying and selling of the manufactured articles that were to be sold in other states, thus implicating the interstate commerce authority of Congress.[50] Despite this limitation on congressional commerce authority, as Currie observes, the courts in this era did not always interpret commerce power narrowly, nor did *Pollock*

---

[47]157 U.S. 429, *modified on rehearing*, 158 U.S. 601 (1895).

[48]David Currie, *The Constitution in the Supreme Court: The Second Century, 188-1986*, p. 25.

[49]156 U.S. 1 (1895).

[50]156 U.S. at 18-19, 34-37.

lead to an assault on federal taxation.[51]

In terms of judicial standards for review of economic regulation, the liberty of contract that the Supreme Court had established in the dicta of *Allgeyer v. Louisiana*[52] in 1897 intellectually correlates with the processing of political economy issues in the 1890s. In light of the 1890s realignment, in fact, the freedom of contract established by the Supreme Court in its holding in *Lochner v. New York*[53], decided in 1905, stood on more credible legal ground, in its day, than the Court in the 1930s may have recognized.[54] *Lochner v. New York* involved the legitimacy of a New York law prohibiting bakery employees from working more than sixty hours per week or ten hours per day in bakeries, for health and safety reasons. Writing for the Court, Justice Rufus W. Peckham finds no legitimate basis, including police power interests, for this regulation and thus declares it an illegitimate interference with the freedom of contract implicitly protected by the Fourteenth Amendment Due Process Clause. The alleged health risks did not pose a "material danger" to workers or to the consumer, he reasoned. He also observes

> no contention that bakers as a class are not equal in intelligence and capacity to men in other trades or manual occupations, or that they are not able to assert their rights and care for themselves without the protecting arm of the State, interfering with their independence of judgment and of action. They are in no sense wards of the State. . . .[55]

---

[51]Currie, p. 29.

[52]165 U.S. 578 (1897).

[53]198 U.S. 45 (1905).

[54]See the retrenchment of judicial scrutiny of economic regulation announced in *Nebbia v. New York*, 291 U.S. 502 (1934) and *West Coast Hotel v. Parrish*, 300 U.S. 379 (1937).

[55]Lochner v. New York, 198 U.S. at 57.

Dissenting, Justice Oliver Wendell Holmes views the case as having been decided pursuant to Herbert Spencer's theory of natural selection and claims that the Constitution does not enact Spencer's theory. "[A] constitution is not intended to embody a particular economic theory, whether of paternalism and the organic relation of the citizen to the State or of laissez faire."[56]

In light of the 1890s realignment, one might acknowledge Justice Holmes's view that the Constitution does not expressly incorporate Spencer's theory of political economy, but also recognize that the political economy developments prior to these elections and the referenda-like nature of these elections lend credence to the suggestion that Spencerian ideology had become a constitutive element of the American polity. As Samuel Eliot Morison observes, Theodore Roosevelt summed up the last quarter of the nineteenth century in the United States quite well:

> A riot of individualistic materialism, under which complete freedom for the individual . . turned out in practice to mean perfect freedom for the strong to wrong the weak. . . . The power of the mighty industrial overlords . . . had increased with giant strides, while the methods controlling them, . . . through the Government, remained archaic and therefore practically impotent."[57]

But in several instances, the Court also upheld state interventions in labor/management relations, leaving pro-industrial "laissez faire" policy an altogether equivocal commitment. In the *Lochner* era, in fact, the Court actually upheld most economic regulations it reviewed, although

---

[56]198 U.S. at 75.

[57]Theodore Roosevelt, Autobiography, quoted in Samuel Eliot Morison, *The Oxford History of the American People: Volume Three, 1869-1963*, (New York: Penguin, 1972), p. 76.

it did declare many regulations unconstitutional.[58] Distinctions used in some of the classic cases of the era suggest the ongoing force of a "laissez faire" ideology protective of industrial interests. Other cases simply defy it. In 1898, for example, the Court sustained a Utah law prohibiting employment in mines, smelters, or ore refineries for more than eight hours per day, based on both legislative findings regarding the health risks to these workers and the observation that mine owners and their employees were not equal in bargaining capacity.[59] In *Muller v. Oregon*[60] the Court sustained an Oregon law limiting female employees in any factory or laundry to a maximum of ten hours per day. The decision was based precisely on what the Court in *Lochner* had not found with respect to bakers: the unequal bargaining power of the protected class of labor. The Court reasoned that women's physical structure placed them at a disadvantaged in the struggle for subsistence, that the well-being of women as future mothers always has been a matter of public interest, and that women always have been dependent on men, and, therefore, protective legislation for women (but not for men) is legitimate.[61] In *Bunting v. Oregon*[62], decided in 1917, the Court sustained an Oregon health measure for workers, which had established a maximum work-day of ten hours, but for three additional hours of overtime at time-and-a-half pay. Here the Court respected the legislative findings regarding the health of the worker and seems to overturn *Lochner* without mentioning the 1905 precedent.

CONCLUDING NOTE: CONSENSUS AND FORMAL

---

[58]For discussion and critique of the "laissez faire" characterization of the Supreme Court at this time, see Roscoe Pound, "Liberty of Contract", 18 *Yale Law Journal* 454 (1909), and Dodd, "Social Legislation and the Courts," 28 *Political Science Quarterly* 1 (1913).

[59]*Holden v. Hardy*, 169 U.S. 366 (1898).

[60]208 U.S. 412 (1908).

[61]208 U.S. at 422-23.

[62]243 U.S. 426 (1917).

AMENDMENT?

The 1890s realignment differs from those studied so far, in terms of constitutional implications, because a major departure from the status quo did not follow it; rather the dominant party of the past emerges even stronger. While it would be too speculative to infer from this an emergent national consensus favoring federal support of industrialization and administration from the 1894-96 realignment, this consolidation of power could help to account for sufficient majoritarian strength across states from 1909 to 1913 responsible for passing the Sixteenth Amendment, which allows for a federal income tax and effectively overruled *Pollock*. Not that concern about state authority in relation to federal authority had diminished, however. The Seventeenth Amendment, which established the direct election of U.S. Senators, also was passed in 1913, and was intended to serve as a means for rehabilitating the place of states in American federalism.[63]

---

[63] *See* William H. Riker, "The Senate and American Federalism," 49 *American Political Science Review* 452 (1955).

6. THE 1930s, SOCIAL WELFARE, ENTITLEMENTS, AND AN ADMINISTRATIVE REPUBLIC

The year 1932 marked the beginning of another major partisan realignment in the United States, as the Democrats, under the leadership of Franklin Roosevelt, usurped the Republicans as the dominant party at both the national and state levels of government. That major policy change accompanied this partisan upheaval is nearly incontrovertible. In both history books and popular discourse, the "New Deal" stands as a turning point in American political development. It also is understood to mark the rise of regulatory or administrative government and the replacement of "dual federalism" with "cooperative federalism". The political scientist Ted Lowi, in fact, marks this era as the early stages of a coming "second Republic of the United States."[1] Yet despite these apparent changes to the polity, the Constitution was not formally amended to reflect them, making the relationship between critical realignments and informal constitutional changes established in previous chapters particularly important for questions regarding the legitimacy of much of the contemporary "welfare", "post-industrial", or "bureaucratic" state.

At least one critic of realignment theory, however, suggests that "realignment" is not the correct term with which to describe the New Deal era, because the partisanship change accompanying it did not result from changes in partisanship affiliation or policy preferences among the pre-existing electorate; rather, partisan upheaval is attributable most directly to the new voters brought into the political process as

---

[1]Theodore J. Lowi, *The End of Liberalism: The Second Republic of the United States*, 2nd ed., (New York: Norton, 1979), p. 273.

Democrats.[2] This argument probably takes semantics a bit too seriously. Irrespective, that is, of the precise cause, a realignment, defined simply as a substantial displacement of the "in-party", did occur in the 1930s. The claim that this realignment largely was the result of the addition of new voters into the electorate, however, is quite well-taken. It seems, in fact, a crucial point, but not as a criticism of realignment theory. Rather, the expansion of "democracy" at this time and the consequences of it may be fundamentally important to an accurate interpretation of the many changes to the American political order that followed the New Deal. They may have a great deal to do with responses to a more inclusive electorate amid a public referendum that unbridled market forces may infringe on the liberty guaranteed to all individuals under classical liberalism.

In order to test this hypothesis, this Chapter applies the two-fold test of informal constitutional amendment applied to realignments in previous chapters.

DID CONSTITUTIONALLY TRANSFORMATIVE PROPOSALS ANIMATE THE 1930S REALIGNMENT?

The Constitutional Status Quo Ante

The roots of the New Deal, as Sidney Milkis observes, lie in the Progressive initiatives of the late nineteenth and early twentieth centuries.[3] As a political theory, "progressivism" was a response to particular social changes wrought by industrialization and the development of "big business" in the latter part of the nineteenth century. American society, that is, traditionally had been structured for community life. Family, church, school, and government generally were part of an integrated community, defined at the local level. Railroads

---

[2]James E. Campbell, "Sources of the New Deal Realignment: The Contributions of Conversion and Mobilization to Partisan Change," 38 *Western Political Quarterly* (September 1985) 357-76.

[3]Sidney M. Milkis, *The President and the Parties: The Transformation of the American Party System Since the New Deal*, (New York: Oxford University Press, 1993).

and industrialization disrupted this traditional way of life by creating new sources of income, involving new work conditions, and often creating a dependency of communities on industries they did not own. Trade associations, unions, and interest groups formed as protective or coping measures.

As the economy changed, much of the population began moving into urban settings, which often served as the centers of emergent finance capitalism. Many of these urban residents were part of the new middle class created by industrialization and finance capitalism. As Robert Wiebe observes, farmers often entered the commercialism fold and came to rely upon wage earners for their farming activities.[4] Merchants and bankers also came to play an important role in shaping economic development.[5] Also clustering in the urban environments, it should be remembered, were immigrants, who proved to be a fertile source of labor.

It is in the cities where progressivism took root. Cities required the provision of various services to meet the needs of their populations, such as fresh water, transportation, sewers, etc. But as communities were transformed by industrialization and big business, groups and neighborhoods that made social action possible also were being destroyed. It was the new middle class, Wiebe explains, that led efforts to forge an order on the social change occurring. Two categories of the middle class, those with strong professional aspirations, such as doctors and lawyers, and those who were specialists in business, labor, and agriculture, sought to improve their professions and tended to view the new social situation as an opportunity for the exercise of their talents.[6] Their increased concern with professionalization and outlets for it, in fact, led not just to the development of professional organizations or economic groupings, but also to political mobilization. For example,

The scientifically minded farmers studied marketing and

---

[4]Robert H. Wiebe, *The Search for Order, 1877-1920*, (New York: Hill and Wang, 1967), p. 16-17.

[5]*Ibid*, pp. 17-27.

[6]*Id.*, p. 112.

suggested novel experiments in government assistance, social workers set their profession in an inclusive urban-industrial framework, and teachers experimented with ways of relating public education to a whole society.[7]

Intellectuals associated with government also began to organize pursuant to a sense of professional purpose. Those within the legal profession, for example, established bar associations. In 1865, social scientists established the American Social Science Association, from which associations centered on various sub-specializations were born.[8]

Politics in this era, however, was intensely partisan, and parochialism kept the parties "a myriad of little units that no one had the capacity--or even the inclination--to combine."[9] Stephen Skowronek explains that efforts to respond to social problems in a unified manner at the national level were precluded by the relationship between state and society fashioned under the original constitutional order:

> The creation of more centralized, stable, and functionally specific institutional connections between state and society was impeded by the tenacity of this highly mobilized, highly competitive, and locally oriented party democracy.[10]

Party machines, Skowronek observes, had gained hold over American institutions and "would have to be broken before new centers of national institutional authority could be built."[11] The power of courts, he adds, grew alongside the power of party machines "to fill the 'void in

---

[7]*Id.*

[8]Stephen Skowronek, *Building a New American State*, p. 43.

[9]Wiebe, p. 28

[10]Skowronek, *Building a New American State*, pp. 39-40.

[11]*Id.*, p. 41.

governance' left between party hegemony and rapid social change."[12]

Those members of the new middle class determined to navigate through this confounding configuration of power in pursuit of uniform reforms were the early "progressives." Wiebe explains:

> . . . The system was so impersonal, so vast, seemingly without beginning or end.
>
> Some sallied forth and returned, licking their wounds, to stay. But the urge to fight again and again infected ever increasing numbers, particularly those from the new middle class. They demanded the right to pursue their ambitions outward rather than simply to be left alone at home, and that in turn required far-reaching social changes. To improve public health, for example, doctors might insist on the renovation of an entire city. Some social workers quite literally called for a new American society. Expansionists in business, labor, agriculture, and the professions, in other words, formulated their interests in terms of continuous policies that necessitated regularity and predictability from unseen thousands.[13]

Urban progressivism, Wiebe observes, centered on a particular discontent: "A patchwork government could no longer manage the range of urban problems with the expertise and economy that articulate citizens now believed they must have."[14] Most progressives sought to take action at governments close to them, and few had access to national power, but "a rudimentary national progressivism was already taking shape around 1900."[15]

"Progressivism," according to Wiebe, "was the central force in a

---

[12]*Id.*

[13]Wiebe, *The Search for Order*, p. 165.

[14]*Id.*, p. 167.

[15]*Id.*, p. 185.

revolution that fundamentally altered the structure of politics and government in the early twentieth century."[16] Progressivism's signature is "administration." An essay written in 1887 by the progressive Woodrow Wilson, according to Sidney Milkis, "marks the first recognition in the United States of public administration as a distinct and separate sphere of government activity."[17] But after 1900, progressives forced government--and even the private sector--to consider the virtues of rational, efficient organization, making optimal use of experts. "Scientific government, the urban reformers believed, would bring opportunity, progress, order, and community."[18] Though not a good example of accomplishment, Wiebe notes, railroad regulation typified the role progressives would have their efforts play in the administration of rates and the storage, transfer, and general handling of cargo.[19] And "one giant firm after another" Wiebe also notes, adopted "some variant of administrative centralization."[20]

The first progressive to animate national politics in the twentieth century as President was Theodore Roosevelt. As Wiebe observes, Roosevelt actively utilized policy experts in his administration pursuant to "the growing demand for public management."[21] Roosevelt helped to pass both the Hepburn Act of 1906, which strengthened the Interstate Commerce Commission, and the Pure Food and Drug Act of 1906, "another experiment in bureaucratic reform."[22] Roosevelt, in fact, utilized the executive office in pursuit of these and other objectives in an unprecedented and distinctively "progressive" manner. Specifically, the

---

[16]*Id.*, p. 181.

[17]Sidney Milkis, *The President and the Parties*, *supra*, n. 3, p. 25.

[18]Wiebe, *The Search for Order*, p. 170.

[19]*Id.*, p. 180.

[20]*Id.*, p. 181.

[21]*Id.*, p. 191.

[22]*Id.*

executive office took the leadership initiative on public policy matters. Wiebe explains:

> Increasingly the important bills, including those to outlaw rebating by the railroads, regulate the food and drug industries, and revise the Sherman Antitrust Act, were either drafted in an executive department or cleared there before they were introduced.[23]

Under Roosevelt's administration, "the executive had assumed the task of studying and resolving the big problems."[24] The President dictated priorities, and the Congress responded to them as lawmakers. But Roosevelt was president only until 1909, and William Howard Taft, his successor, did not pursue a progressive agenda.

The 1912 campaign for the presidency, however, witnessed the rival progressive campaigns of Woodrow Wilson, running as a Democrat, and Theodore Roosevelt, who now was running as a Progressive Party candidate. The campaign, as Milkis observes, distinguished between two versions of progressivism, which are particularly important for understanding the progressivism incorporated into the New Deal of the 1930s. The chief distinguishing issue was national administrative power. Roosevelt viewed big corporations as legitimate market actors but subject to strict public control through regulation by a powerful trade commission.[25] The Progressive Party platform in 1912, moreover, suggests that the reforms to be carried out required the destruction of the traditional party system.[26] Wilson advocated the freeing of business from the plague of monopoly and special privilege, so as to make unnecessary the dangerous centralization of power implicated by national regulatory

---

[23]*Id.*, p. 191.

[24]*Id.*, p. 193.

[25]Milkis, *The President and the Parties*, p. 35.

[26]Id., p. 31.

structures.[27] More importantly, perhaps, Wilson sought to achieve reform within and through the existing party system, which had come to impede development of a strong nation-state. Wilson believed that parties and Congress could be made to adopt progressive measures through effective executive leadership. As Milkis observes, "[It] was necessary to strengthen the role of the president as party leader so that the executive as the leader of national opinion could fuse the executive and legislative branches in his own person."[28] Jeffrey Tulis, in fact, has demonstrated that Wilson favored bringing the president "into more intimate contact with Congress and the people"[29] for the purpose of exercising leadership that would raise politics "to the level of rational disputation."[30]

Wilson, of course, won the election. In his first year in office, Wilson helped to reconstruct the national banking and currency system by securing the passage of the Federal Reserve Act, which created a federal reserve bank in each of twelve districts across the country and the Federal Reserve Board, which controls the discount rates charged to the federal reserve banks. Wilson, according to Milkis, gradually moved toward policies more accepting of national administration, such as the Federal Trade Commission, established in 1914. Wilson and Congress also enacted into law a rural credits law, a worker's compensation act for the federal civil service, and a child labor law. Wilson also moved to strengthen the role of the President within the party. In his first Annual Message to Congress, in fact, he urged the adoption of a national presidential primary.[31] He also revised the practice of appearing before Congress to deliver the State of the Union address.[32]

---

[27]Id., p. 35.

[28]Id., p. 28.

[29]Jeffrey K. Tulis, *The Rhetorical Presidency* (Princeton: Princeton University Press, 1987), p. 128.

[30]*Id.* , p. 129.

[31]*Id.*, pp. 28-29.

[32]*Id.*, p. 30.

Upon conclusion of World War I, into which he reluctantly led the United States, Wilson also sought to lead the United States into an international peace-keeping association, the League of Nations, which may be seen as consistent with the progressive objective of subjecting selected political matters to rational organization and rational deliberation, despite Theodore Roosevelt's denouncement of the plan. Wilson's stated objective seems simple. "My one object in promoting the League of Nations is to prevent future wars," he reportedly told George Clemenceau, the French prime minister.[33]   Wilson's failure to secure ratification of the treaty enacting the League of Nations in the U.S. Senate is well-known.   Less well-known and perhaps important for understanding the breadth of the New Deal and post-New Deal changes in the American polity is the remainder of Wilson's reported conversation with Clemenceau. Clemenceau suggested to Wilson that war cannot be prevented unless all nations agree on three fundamental principles, the declaration and enforcement of racial equality, the freedom of immigration, and global free trade.   On the race question, Wilson apparently replied, "The race question is very touchy in the United States, and the Southern and West Coast senators would defeat any treaty containing such a clause."[34]   On the immigration matter, Wilson reportedly observed that "my country is determined to exclude Orientals absolutely, and Congress is already considering restrictions on European immigration."[35] On the question of free trade: "I personally would like to see it, and my party has lowered the American tariff; but I could never get Congress to agree to a customs union with Europe, Asia, and Africa."[36] The racial equality matter will be revisited when discussing Franklin Roosevelt's progressive administration.

Warren Harding successfully campaigned for the presidency with the

---

[33]Samuel Eliot Morison, *The Oxford History of the American People: Volume Three, 1869-1963*, (New York: Mentor, 1972, originally 1965), pp. 209-10.

[34]*Ibid*, p. 210.

[35]*Id.*

[36]*Id.*

pledge of a "return to normalcy", an end to the flurry of progressive regulation that had characterized the previous decades. During the Harding and Coolidge administrations, various regulatory agencies remained in place, but few new ones were created; and agencies that might have staved off the economic crash of 1929, such as the Federal Reserve Board and Federal Trade Commission, Samuel Morison argues, did not act to do so, because they had been "diluted by political hacks or Republican financiers who did not believe in the regulative functions which they were supposed to perform."[37] Thus the rise in security prices that began in 1923 was allowed to reach a "giddy height" in 1925, and a "general euphoria drew more and more 'suckers' into the speculative market."[38] Corporations proliferated, as did stock pools. By October of 1929, banks had made loans in the amount of $8.5 billion for speculation. While a few warned of a coming tragedy, President Coolidge suggested the present and future be regarded with optimism. In 1928, presidential candidate Herbert Hoover observed that "the day when poverty will be banished from this nation" was in sight.[39]

When the Great Depression occurred, Hoover, who had some progressive leanings,[40] aimed to relieve the suffering by encouraging charity, but not by endorsing federal direct relief, which traditionally was the prerogative of state and local governments. As Sundquist observes, Hoover expected the Depression to be brief and told Congress in 1930 that "[e]conomic depression cannot be cured by legislative action or executive pronouncement."[41] In January of 1932, Hoover signed into a

---

[37]*Id.*, p. 282.

[38]*Id.*, p. 282.

[39]*Id.*, p. 285.

[40]*See* Stephen Skowronek, *The Politics Presidents Make: Leadership from John Adams to George Bush* (Cambridge: Harvard University Press, 1993), pp. 265-70.

[41]Quoted in James Sundquist, *Dynamics of the Party System: Alignment and Realignment of Political Parties in the United States*, rev. ed., (Washington: Brookings, 1983), p. 200.

progressive measure, the Reconstruction Finance Corporation, which lent money to railroads, banks, and other interests. But Hoover refused either to exercise or advertise his progressive leanings much beyond this, according to Skowronek, because he owed his political livelihood to the more conservative political elements.[42] In the 1932 national elections, the progressives captured the Democratic Party, and the party's presidential nominee himself was a progressive.[43] The Democrats won big, and ushered in enduring partisan displacement.

Constitutionally Transformative Issues:

1. The legitimacy of federal governmental management of market outcomes.

Despite the economic malaise of the country in the early 1930s, the Republicans remained steadfast in their belief in a self-correcting economy and dangers of attempts to legislate an end to the depression. Sundquist notes that the division between the Republicans and progressive Democrats over a proposed national system of employment exchanges, fashioned on preexisting state and local public employment agencies and supported by federal monies, in 1930 "signaled, in both tone and content, the terms of the party struggle over the role of the federal government that was to dominate national politics for the rest of the depression decade and continue for half a century afterward."[44] Democratic Senator from New York Robert F. Wagner, who sponsored the unemployment bill, lamented the "waste of human life which is the price of demoralizing unemployment" and reasoned that unemployment lies within the purview of federal authority "because many of the remedies to be applied can only be applied by national agencies."[45] Conservatives charged that the bill was unconstitutional and that, if

---

[42]Skowronek, *The Politics Presidents Make*, pp. 269-70.

[43]For details, *see* James L. Sundquist, *Dynamics of the Party System*, ch. 10.

[44]Sundquist, *Dynamics of the Party System*, p. 201.

[45]Quoted in Sundquist, *Dynamics of the Party System, p. 201* (citing *Congressional Record*, April 28, 1930, pp. 797-98).

implemented, it would destroy the incentive for individuals to take part in self-government.[46] When the bill passed Congress, President Hoover pocket-vetoed it, claiming that the measure proposed "the most vicious tyranny ever set up in the United States."[47]

Precisely what Franklin Roosevelt and the Democrats had in mind, in terms of federal government intervention, became, of course, much clearer once Roosevelt became President and the Democrats regained control of Congress. The first hundred days of Roosevelt's administration witnessed many legislative and executive initiatives in response to the economic crisis. Passed in record time, for example, the Emergency Banking Act reopened banks under a system of licenses and conservators and aimed to prevent the hoarding of gold. Perhaps the most important action in Roosevelt's first term was his executive order, in 1933, for the U.S. to abandon the gold standard, which Morison describes as the "most revolutionary act of the New Deal . . ."[48] Among other measures passed were: the Civilian Conservation Corps, which, by the expiration of the program, gave about two million men work helping to conserve natural resources; the Federal Emergency Relief Act, a component of which was the Civil Works Administration, which provided direct relief through work opportunities building roads, schoolhouses, and airports; the Agricultural Adjustment Act, which authorized the Agriculture Department to reduce the planting of staple commodities and reduce the breeding of pigs and meat cattle, and which raised national farm income substantially. As these measures were implemented, resistance to this brand of progressivism took a more definite shape.

2. Executively-driven federal intervention into state and local economic activity related to, but not the same as, interstate commerce.

When the U.S. Supreme Court had reviewed a federal commercial ban

---

[46]Sundquist, *Dynamics of the Party System*, p. 201.

[47]*Id.*, p. 202.

[48]Morison, *The Oxford History of the American People*, p. 304.

on products of child labor in *Hammer v. Dagenhart*[49] in 1918, it set forth, in no uncertain terms, the constitutional principle that Congress did not possess the authority to prohibit the transportation in interstate commerce of goods manufactured by child labor, because the object of the ban is manufacturing, which is not interstate commerce; rather it is a "purely local matter to which the federal authority does not extend."[50] Some of Roosevelt's New Deal program, however, in particular the National Industrial Recovery Act (NIRA), reached into matters traditionally considered state and local and was premised on federal interstate commerce authority, which made for many constitutional challenges, several of which were successful.

The Supreme Court, for example, in 1935 declared unconstitutional the NIRA, just as the Act's term was about to expire, following administrative difficulties that had beleaguered it. One issue regarding the NIRA in *Schechter Poultry Corp. v. United States*,[51] were convictions under the Act for violating one of its codes regarding wage, hour, and trade practices, which, opponents charged, were intrastate activities and therefore beyond federal commerce power. Chief Justice Evan Hughes, in his majority opinion, reasons that the activities in question were not transactions in interstate commerce, nor did they directly affect interstate commerce. While manufacturing activities that have a direct effect on interstate commerce could be the legitimate object of federal commerce power,[52] he notes, the wages and hours here have only an indirect effect on interstate commerce. They therefore remain solely within the domain of state power. He added:

> If the commerce clause were construed to reach all enterprises and transactions which could be said to have an indirect effect

---

[49]247 U.S. 251 (1918).

[50]247 U.S. at 276.

[51]295 U.S. 495 (1935).

[52]295 U.S. at 546-48, with the reference being to the ruling in *Houston E. & W. Texas Railway Co. v. United States* (The Shreveport Rate Case), 234 U.S. 342 (1914).

upon interstate commerce, the federal authority would embrace practically all the activities of the people and the authority of the State over its domestic concerns would exist only by sufferance of the federal government.[53]

For similar reasons, the Supreme Court also declared the Bituminous Coal Conservation Act of 1935 unconstitutional in *Carter v. Carter Coal Co.*[54] in 1936. At issue in the case were maximum hour and minimum wage regulations under a national bituminous coal code. Again the Court found such matters part of production and not interstate commerce. The Court, in deference to precedent, acknowledged that a manufacturing activity that has a direct effect on interstate commerce potentially could lie within federal commerce authority, but the evils that arise from the struggles between employers and employees over "wages, working conditions, the right of collective bargaining, etc.," Justice George Sutherland reasons, "are all local evils over which the federal government has no legislative control."[55]

Roosevelt's progressive belief in the necessity of strong executive leadership in a rationally-structured bureaucracy that makes use of experts was also subjected to constitutional challenge. The NIRA authorized the President to formulate regulatory codes for various industries. In *Schechter Poultry Co.*, however, the Supreme Court, in addition to finding that the act exceeded federal authority under the interstate commerce clause, also rejected this congressional delegation of authority to the executive branch, finding it "virtually unfettered" authority and therefore in violation of the separation of powers under the Constitution.[56]

These cases, however, should not be understood as evidence that the Supreme Court stood opposed to all regulation of the economy at this

---

[53]295 U.S. at 546.

[54]298 U.S. 238 (1936).

[55]298 U.S. at 308.

[56]*Schechter Poultry Corp. v. United States*, 295 U.S. at 542.

time. In 1934, the Court sustained a minimum price for milk set by a New York Milk Control Board, a state agency, against the charge that the price fixing violated the federal due process guarantee.[57] In the same year, the Court also sustained a Minnesota law that granted temporary relief from mortgage foreclosures and real estate sales, against a charge that the legislation violated the contract clause. The Court reasoned that the legislation altered no substantial right pursuant to the contract, but that an emergency situation had given rise to the state's legitimate exercise of police power to delay temporarily the enforcement of the contracts in question.[58]

Even so, the President's reelection campaign in 1936, and his success in it, may explain the degree to which he aimed to modify the paradigmatic conception of the federal government--and may also explain the severity of his response to the setback to the New Deal levied by the Supreme Court: his court-packing plan. Roosevelt's commitment to expansive administration did not rest comfortably with party politics, Milkis observes, but he did not favor abandonment of the party system altogether. Milkis suggests he "believed that leadership within the traditional two-party framework was necessary to organize public opinion into a governing coalition." Roosevelt himself, in fact, drafted the Democratic Party platform, offering a redefinition of the "self-evident" rights announced in the Declaration of Independence.

> We hold this truth to be self-evident–that government in a modern civilization has certain inescapable obligations to its citizens, among which are:
>
> 1. Protection of the family and home.
> 2. Establishment of a democracy of opportunity for all the people.
> 3. Aid to those overtaken by disaster. These obligations, neglected through twelve years of the old leadership, have once more been recognized by American government. Under the new

---

[57]*Nebbia v. New York*, 291 U.S. 502 (1934).

[58]*Home Building & Loan Association v. Blaisdell*, 290 U.S. 398 (1934).

leadership they will never be neglected.[59]

The platform included a provision on the Social Security Act, declaring it a foundation for a "structure of economic security for all our people, making sure that this benefit shall keep step with the ever-increasing capacity of America to provide a high standard of living for all its citizens."[60] By their platform, as Milkis notes, the Republicans claimed they would preserve political liberty.[61] Roosevelt won the election in a landslide.

In the February after his electoral triumph, moreover, Roosevelt presented to Congress a federal judiciary reorganization plan that would allow him to add one justice to the Supreme Court for each justice on the Court over the age of seventy who did not retire. This effort to authorize Roosevelt to "pack" the Court with staunch supporters of the New Deal drew considerable political and legal fire, and the bill failed. But the pressure on the Court apparently effected a jurisprudential "switch in time that saved nine." Less than two months after the court-packing bill, the Court decided *West Coast Hotel Co. v. Parrish*[62], which overruled a 1923 decision that, on the ground that Nineteenth Amendment had made women and men virtually equal, invalidated a minimum wage law for women. In *West Coast Hotel Co.*, the Court reasoned that "the liberty safeguarded [by the Constitution] is liberty in a social organization which requires the protection of law against the evils which menace the health, safety, morals and welfare of the people."[63] The Court also commented on the exploitation of workers:

---

[59]Quoted in Sidney Milkis, *The President and the Parties*, pp. 48-49, citing "Democratic Platform of 1936", in Donald Bruce Johnson ed., *National Party Platforms*, (Urbana: University of Illinois Press, 1978).

[60]*Id.*, p. 49.

[61]*Id.*, p. 49.

[62]300 U.S. 379 (1937).

[63]300 U.S. at 391.

The exploitation of a class of workers who are in an unequal position with respect to bargaining power and are thus relatively defenseless against the denial of a living wage is not only detrimental to their health and well being but casts a direct burden for their support upon the community. What these workers lose in wages the taxpayers are called upon to pay. . . . The community is not bound to provide what is in effect a subsidy for unconscionable employers. The community may direct its law-making power to correct the abuse which springs from their selfish disregard of the public interest. . . .[64]

Shortly after *West Coast Hotel*, the Supreme Court decided the watershed case, *National Labor Relations Board v. Jones & Laughlin Steel Corp.*[65] At issue in the case was the National Labor Relations Act, which prohibited unfair labor practices affecting commerce and defined "commerce" and "affecting commerce" more broadly than allowed in, for example, *Adkins v. Children's Hospital*[66], which had struck down a minimum wage law for women, and *Hammer v. Dagenhart*. The Act had defined "commerce" as "trade, traffic, commerce, transportation, or communication among the several States" and "affecting commerce" as "in commerce, or burdening or obstructing commerce or the free flow of commerce, or having led to tending to lead to a labor dispute burdening or obstructing commerce or the free flow of commerce." In sustaining the Act, Chief Justice Hughes reasoned that

. . . the power to regulate commerce is the power to enact "all appropriate legislation" for its "protection and advancement." . . . That power is plenary and may be exerted to protect interstate commerce "no matter what the source of the dangers which threaten it." . . . Although activities may be intrastate in character when separately considered, if they have such a close and substantial relation to interstate commerce that their control is essential or appropriate to protect that commerce from

---

[64]300 U.S. at 399-400.

[65]301 U.S. 1 (1937).

[66]261 U.S. 525 (1923).

burdens or obstructions, Congress cannot be denied the power to exercise that control.[67]

Hughes was not insensitive to federalism, however. He noted that this scope of power must be considered "in light of our dual system of government" and could not be extended so as to "obliterate the distinction between what is national and what is local."[68]

In 1938, in *United States v. Carolene Products Co.*[69], moreover, the Court reviewed the Filled Milk Act of 1923, in which Congress had declared its finding that "filled milk"–milk from which natural milk fat has been extracted–is an "adultered" food and "injurious to the public health", and prohibited the shipment of filled milk in interstate commerce. The Court reasoned that it should defer to declared congressional findings of facts supporting the legislation, and that

> Even in the absence of such aids the existence of facts supporting the legislative judgment is to be presumed, for regulatory legislation affecting ordinary commercial transactions is not to be pronounced unconstitutional unless in the light of the facts made known or generally assumed it is such a character as to preclude the assumption that it rests upon some rational basis.
> . . .[70]

Roosevelt, it should be noted, also used executive authority to improve economic opportunities for groups whose opportunities under the previous regime generally had been marginal. Roosevelt's Secretary of the Interior, Harold Ickes, successfully urged Congress to pass, in 1934, the Indian Reorganization Act, which reversed a sharp decline in tribal land holdings. Roosevelt also abolished segregation in federal offices in

---

[67]*NLRB v. Jones & Laughlin Steel Corp.*, 301 U.S. at 37.

[68]Critics of the post-New Deal constitutional order typically argue that such an obliteration between what is national and what is local has occurred

[69] 304 U.S. 144 (1938).

[70] 304 U.S. at 152.

of 1941, following his election to a third term of office and facing the charge that federal money pouring into defense plants was subsidizing discrimination, Roosevelt issued Executive Order 8802, which established a Committee on Fair Employment Practices. Under these Practices, employers and unions were prohibited from discrimination on the basis of race, creed, color, or national origin.[71]

3. The Interchangeability of executive agreements and treaties

Bruce Ackerman and David Golove have demonstrated that public debate and national elections in the 1940s focused attention on the constitutional legitimacy of the interchangeability of executive agreements with treaties.[72] Under the original Constitution, the President must submit proposed treaties to the Senate, who may ratify the treaty with a two-thirds majority vote of those present. At the outset of World War II, there was considerable debate over the traditional American policy of isolationism versus the view that this policy's manifestation in the treaty ratification requirement precludes the role in international affairs the United States must play. Many Americans, that is, remained opposed to international commitments or alliances with foreign countries, and the two-thirds rule served to make such commitments or alliances relatively difficult to secure. It defeated the Treaty of Versailles. Many also believed that a greater American role in international affairs was the only way to avoid a third world war.[73]

As World War II progressed, Ackerman and Golove observe, public opinion shifted sharply in favor of multilateral internationalism, and both scholars and journalists were exploring the possibility of amending the Constitution's two-thirds rule.[74] By the 1944 presidential election, both

---

[71]*See* William Manchester, *The Glory and the Dream: A Narrative History of America, 1932-1972*, (Toronto: Bantam, 1975), p. 244.

[72]Bruce Ackerman and David Golove, "Is NAFTA Constitutional?", 108 *Harvard Law Review* 799 (1995).

[73]*Ibid*, p. 862, n. 283.

[74]*Id.*, pp. 862-73.

Constitution's two-thirds rule.[74] By the 1944 presidential election, both parties favored internationalism, but the Republican platform stipulated that the Charter of the United Nations be submitted to the Senate as a treaty. The Democrats favored more flexible requirements for the ratification of treaties.[75]

Roosevelt won the election, and isolationists in the Senate lost dramatically. As a result, the House of Representatives began deliberations on a proposed constitutional amendment, which would have substituted a majority vote in Congress for the two-thirds vote in the Senate rule. Apparently not wanting to destroy the bipartisan internationalist consensus that had been built, Roosevelt elected not to wage a formal amendment battle with Senate Republicans over the two-thirds rule. Rather, he attempted to forge a compromise that would accomplish the same objective of "interchangeability" of executive agreements and treaties. The Administration, in fact, already had begun the process of legitimating interchangeability by tentatively sending agreements to Congress rather than the Senate. In brief, the compromise was that the President would send the United Nations Charter to the Senate as a treaty, in exchange for the Senate's approval. The Senate also allowed the President to submit virtually all other elements of the post-War plans as congressional-executive agreements. By the late 1940s, interchangeability had been established.[76]

DID ANY TRANSFORMATIVE POLICIES HAVE WIDESPREAD SUPPORT BEYOND THE REALIGNING ERA?

On the Partisan Composition of the Electorate

Long-term, transformative changes associated with the New Deal first may be gleaned from the scope of the partisanship changes to the electorate and the state of the parties in the decades afterward. In 1932, Roosevelt advocated the development of an economic bill of rights. In

---

[74]*Id.*, pp. 862-73.

[75]*Id.*, pp. 883-89

[76]*Id.*, pp. 889-96.

pursuit of these objectives, however, would require the development of national, executively-driven administrative capacities capable of transcending the local organization and initiatives of the party system-- that is, would require the diminution of the role parties would play in the process of government. Roosevelt's effort to strengthen his objectives for the party and the executive office include his effort to unseat several conservative Democrats in 1938 and the Executive Reorganization Act of 1939.[77]

Thus the Democratic Party became recognized as the "active-government" party. It also became the majority party in the country and remains so to date. The Democrats also gained control of both houses of Congress and, over the past several decades, usually have had control of both the House of Representative and the Senate. Table 6.1 demonstrates the congressional losses suffered by the Republicans at the outset of the realignment and the governing power that the Democrats have had in Congress since the New Deal era. Perhaps even more important, the ideological differences between the two parties seemed to have narrowed substantially in the decades after the 1930s realignment. President Lyndon Johnson's Great Society programs of the 1960s expanded further the New Deal philosophy and techniques of government, making partisan differences even more a matter of degree of commitment to this philosophy of government, not one of its legitimacy. With this development, it seems, has come an increased public perception of the irrelevance of political parties, as Martin Wattenberg has demonstrated,[78] which, to the extent partisanship reveals strongly competing ideologies is an outcome might would not have bothered Franklin Roosevelt too much.[79]

---

[77] *See* Milkis, *The President and the Parties*, pp. 123-24 and ch. 6.

[78] *See* Martin P. Wattenberg, *The Decline of American Political Parties, 1952-1984*, (Cambridge: Harvard University Press, 1986).

[79] *See* Sidney M. Milkis, *The President and the Parties*, pp. 44-51.

Table 6.1*

Year	Congress	House of Reps.		Senate	
		Rep.	Dem.	Rep.	Dem.
1921-23	67th	301	131	59	37
1923-25	68th	225	205	51	43
1925-27	69th	247	183	56	39
1927-29	70th	237	195	49	46
1929-31	71st	267	167	56	39
1931-33	72nd	220	214	48	47
1933-35	73rd	117	310	35	60
1935-37	74th	103	319	25	69
1937-39	75th	89	331	16	76
1939-41	76th	164	261	23	69
1941-43	77th	162	268	28	66
1943-45	78th	208	218	37	58
1945-47	79th	190	242	38	56
1947-49	80th	245	188	51	45
1949-51	81st	171	263	42	54
1951-53	82nd	199	234	47	49
1953-55	83rd	221	211	48	47
1955-57	84th	203	232	47	48
1957-59	85th	200	233	47	49

*Source: U.S. Bureau of the Census, *Historical Statistics of the United States: Colonial Times to 1957*, (Washington, 1960).

Specific long-term policy transformations--

1. Federal Intervention into the Economy

The most important, enduring development regarding federal interstate commerce power following New Deal politics was that the courts effectively began to defer to congressional judgments on questions of when regulation is legitimate. Though not removed from the "switch in time" politics of the 1930s, two Supreme Court cases of the 1940s are even clearer departures from the traditional understanding of federal commerce power than were *West Coast Hotel* or *Jones & Laughlins Steel Corp.* At issue in *United States v. Darby*[80] was the manufacturing/commerce distinction, this time arising in the context of the Fair Labor Standards Act of 1938, with regard specifically to a prohibition of proscribed goods from shipment in interstate commerce and to wage and hour requirements. With regard to the prohibition of particular goods, the Court noted that the fact that the prohibition is intended to restrict intrastate use of articles of commerce, or has the effect of doing so, is irrelevant to whether congressional authority is legitimate. "It is no objection to the assertion of the power to regulate interstate commerce that its exercise is attended by the same incidents which attend the exercise of the police power of the states."[81] Regarding the wage and hour restrictions, the Court observed that federal interstate commerce power

> is not confined to the regulation of commerce among the states. It extends to those activities intrastate which so affect interstate commerce or the exercise of the power of Congress over it as to make regulation of them appropriate means to the attainment of a legitimate end, the exercise of the granted power of Congress to regulate interstate commerce. . . .[82]

In *Wickard v. Filburn*[83], the Court reviewed the legitimacy of the Secretary of Agriculture's penalty on a farmer for having grown wheat in excess of his allotment under the Agricultural Adjustment Act, despite the wheat having been grown not for sale but for consumption on his farm. From the perspective of the Act, the wheat was "available for marketing." The following passage from the majority opinion illustrates the collapse of the manufacturing/commerce distinction that had served to support "dual federalism":

---

[80]312 U.S. 100 (1941).

[81]312 U.S. at 114.

[82]312 U.S. at 118.

[83]317 U.S. 111 (1942).

marketing." The following passage from the majority opinion illustrates the collapse of the manufacturing/commerce distinction that had served to support "dual federalism":

> That an activity is of local character . . . might help in determining whether in the absence of Congressional action it would be permissible for the state to exert its power on the subject matter, even though in so doing it to some degree affected interstate commerce. But even if appellee's activity be local and though it may not be regarded as commerce, it may still, whatever its nature, be reached by Congress if it exerts a substantial economic effect on interstate commerce, and this irrespective of whether such effect is what might at some earlier time have been defined as "direct" or "indirect."[84]

Under constitutional law, the expansive reach of congressional authority pursuant to the interstate commerce clause has endured into the recent decades. The 1960s and even early 1970s, in fact, witnessed a new wave of active-government initiatives, many of which relied on the constitutional order borne in the New Deal--the War on Poverty, the Occupational Safety, and Health Administration and the Environmental Protection Agency, for example. Even the prohibition of racial discrimination in places of public accommodation under the Civil Rights Act of 1964, moreover, was sustained as legitimate congressional protection of interstate commerce.[85] Even in more conservative 1985, in *Garcia v. San Antonio Metropolitan Transit Authority*[86], the Court affirmed the power of Congress to enforce minimum-wage and overtime provisions of the Fair Labor Standards Act against states "in areas of traditional governmental functions."[87] In this case, in fact, the Court

---

[84]317 U.S. at 124-25.

[85]*See Heart of Atlanta Motel v. United States*, 379 U.S. 241 (1964); *Katzenbach v. McClung*, 379 U.S. 294 (1964).

[86]469 U.S. 528 (1985).

[87]469 U.S. at 530 (quoting *National League of Cities v. Usery*, 426 U.S. 833, 852 (1976)).

will not be promulgated."[88]

2. Executive Agreements

A general consensus on the legal interchangeability of executive agreements with treaties, Ackerman and Glove suggest, was established by the end of the 1940s. Perhaps the best example of its enduring nature, Ackerman and Glove also note, is the inattention to a question of constitutionality regarding the North American Free Trade Agreement (NAFTA), which was approved by a simply majority vote in Congress. But they concede, the consensus has frayed recently, particularly during debate over the new General Agreement on Trade and Tariffs (GATT). Indeed, Laurence Tribe vociferously has denounced the constitutionality of a bicameral procedure for approving the new World Trade Organization.

4. Subsequent transformation by inference: Brown, Griswold, and the Bill of Rights

Amid the developments in American federalism and political economy that followed the 1930s realignment came two decisions by the U.S. Supreme Court, *Brown v. Board of Education*[89] and *Griswold v. Connecticut*,[90] which, as Bruce Ackerman observes, seem distinctive departures from traditional higher law, but not clearly manifestations of the transformative politics that characterized the 1930s or the 1860s.[91] These decisions involved matters of racial equality and sexual freedom, respectively, and today stand as critical developments in constitutional doctrine pertaining to racial justice and non-textually-based individual rights. As Ackerman notes, moreover, parallels exist between the two

---

[88]*Garcia v. San Antonio Metropolitan Transit Authority*, 469 U.S. at 556; *see also* 468 U.S. at 547-57.

[89]347 U.S. 483 (1954).

[90]381 U.S. 479 (1965).

[91]Bruce A. Ackerman, *We the People: Foundations*, (Cambridge: Harvard University Press), pp. 133-140.

These decisions involved matters of racial equality and sexual freedom, respectively, and today stand as critical developments in constitutional doctrine pertaining to racial justice and non-textually-based individual rights. As Ackerman notes, moreover, parallels exist between the two cases that make them analytically interesting:

> Racial equality, sexual freedom: these ideals are very different in their philosophical justification and doctrinal elaboration. And yet, when we step back to questions of constitutional process, parallels emerge. In each case, the Justices destabilized traditional values with deep roots in the folkways of the country; in each case, they were accused of imposing the values of the Eastern liberal establishment without interpretive warrant in the Constitution; in each case, many of the Court's defenders implicitly conceded this charge by depicting the Justices as the nation's moral leaders; in each case, the Court's more legalistic supporters gave low grades to the opinions in *Brown* and *Griswold* and searched for better arguments that might buttress these contested decisions.[92]

Does the study of realignments in relation to constitutional development provide any useful interpretive perspective here? The answer, it seems, is "yes," because of particular events concerning racial inequities that occurred during the realigning years and the increased American commitment to international security and the consolidated nature of the American state that emerged from the New Deal era. Attention to *Griswold*, moreover, may even provide some perspective for understanding the "incorporation" of most Bill of Rights provisions into the Fourteenth Amendment limitations against the states.

–Brown as an Inference from the Realignment

The racial equality development of *Brown*, to be begin with, is less disconnected from the realignment of the 1930s in light of the movement toward a more equitable treatment of racial minorities begun by the Roosevelt Administration. As noted earlier in this Chapter, positive developments occurred in regard to both Native Americans, such as the

---

[92]*Id.*

Indian Reorganization Act, and African Americans, such as the abolition of segregation in federal offices.   Roosevelt had promised a regime of more democratic opportunity, and efforts to bring groups previously on the margins of economic and social opportunity more into the mainstream of such possibilities demonstrates some realization of the promise. Even though racial equality had not been processed as one of the constitutionally transformative issues of the 1930s, the matter was attached to the transformation as it evolved. It bears a logical relationship to the idea of a more inclusive, democratic regime. It also lends credibility to the United States as a leader of the "Free (non-racist) World"[93], which seems one of the points Clemenceau made to Wilson, in his explanation of the three requisites for securing international peace.[94] Thus, even if the Supreme Court had little doctrinal warrant for *Brown v. Board of Education*, the Progressive politics animating the New Deal suggest a political warrant via popular referendum or logical inference from it.

Brown therefore makes perfect sense, precisely as Bruce Ackerman has suggested, as an interpretive act, rather than "a prophecy." It can be understood as an effort to integrate racial equality more fully into the progressive program endorsed in the 1930s, which, as it was implemented, had moved toward greater socio-economic inclusiveness. In its famous footnote number four to the *United States v. Carolene Products* decision of 1938, the Supreme Court, in fact, announced that prejudice against discrete and insular minorities may affect the political processes such that heightened judicial scrutiny of these prejudices may be required.   The disparaging effects of segregation upon African-American schoolchildren on government-sponsored education, in fact, is the focus of the analysis in *Brown*. In *Brown*, Chief Justice Warren observes that among children in grade and high schools racial segregation "generates a feeling of inferiority as to their status in the community that may affect their hearts and minds in a way unlikely ever

---

[93]*See* Mary Dudziak, "Desegregation as a Cold War Imperative," *Stanford Law Review* 41:61 (1988) (maintaining that anti-communism interests played an important role in desegregation in the United States).

[94]*See supra*, n. 33 and accompanying text.

are consistent with precedent upholding "progressive" analyses of the public interest in the effects of conditions on particular groups of people imposed on them because of their subordinate status. In 1911, for example, in *Baltimore & Ohio R. Co. v. Interstate Commerce Commission*[96], the Supreme Court upheld a limitation on the hours of railroad employees, following an analysis of the harm to a state interest implicated in longs hours worked by railroad employees:

> The length of hours of service has a direct relation to the efficiency of the human agencies upon which protection to life and property necessarily depends. . . . In its power suitably to provide for the safety of employees and travelers, Congress was not limited to the enactment of laws relating to mechanical appliances, but it was also competent to consider, and to endeavor to reduce, the dangers incident to the strain of excessive hours of duty on the part of engineers, conductors, train dispatchers, telegraphers, and other persons embraced within the class defined by this act.   And in imposing restrictions having reasonable relation to this end there is no interference with liberty of contract as guaranteed by the Constitution.[97]

In 1937, in *West Coast Hotel v. Parrish*, the Court found a legitimate state interest in the health of women "and their protection from unscrupulous and overreaching employers." The Court, in fact, observed that the state legislature was entitled to consider that women's

> bargaining power is relatively weak, and that they are the ready victims of those who would take advantage of their necessitous circumstances. The legislature was entitled to adopt measure to reduce the evils of the 'sweating system,' the exploiting of workers at wages so low as to be insufficient to meet the bare cost of living, thus making their very helplessness the occasion

---

[96]221 U.S. 612 (1911).

[97]221 U.S. at 619.

of a most injurious competition.[98]

–*Griswold as Inference from the Realignment*

When considering the place of *Griswold* in the post-New Deal era, it is important to reflect on the constitutional understanding of the proper allocation of power between the federal and state governments prior to 1937 and the decisions of *West Coast Hotel v. Parrish* and *National Labor Relations Board v. Jones & Laughlin Steel Corp.* The scope of the national government's power then was understood to be express in and limited by the text of the Constitution, with the states and "the people themselves" having all remaining authority. The commerce clause, however open it may be to interpretation from today's perspective, generally was not understood to empower the national government to reach into affairs traditionally the subject of state and local authority.[99] The New Deal transformations, of course, changed this balance of power. The national government and government generally came to play a greater number of roles in people's lives. But with this expansion of power came new opportunities for government to infringe on liberties that could be or previously were understood to be "off limits."

One of the concerns logically emanating from this expansion of governmental authority is the individual's sense of privacy, especially in relation to the capacity of government to shape thought processes. In the context of contemporary governmental power to communicate ideas and thereby shape the otherwise private domain of belief, for example, Mark Yudof cites several reasons to examine the limits of this power to communicate:

> Increasingly, government communication is an element of public policy. Government does not simply run the public household, providing goods and services, or order private affairs by direct regulation, subjecting people to imprisonment, fines, taxes, physical coercion, and civil liability in order to accomplish public objectives. Government also seeks to gain

---

[98]300 U.S. 379, 398-99 (1979).

[99]*E.g., Hammer v. Dagenhart*, 247 U.S. 251 (1918).

compliance with rules and policies by persuading people of their rightness, of the advantages of voluntary compliance, and of the risks of alternative modes of action. It seeks to arouse peer pressure against individuals who deviate. It seeks to educate and to rehabilitate. The greater government's ability to reach mass audiences and to communicate successfully with those audiences, the greater the potential for effective implementation of government policy.[100]

In the context of expansive and perhaps pervasive governmental power, one's right of privacy would seem to arise as a legitimate interest, as would most of the fundamental rights contemplated originally only in the context of an altogether decentralized system of government. Hence the legitimacy, one might argue, of placing the privacy issue in *Griswold*, which involved a statute criminalizing the use of contraception between married people, in the context of twentieth-century active government, which seems to be what the majority opinion does in *Griswold*. In his majority opinion, Justice William Douglas first cites to several non-textual rights that have been protected by the Court in the twentieth-century and then finds penumbral rights of privacy associated with guarantees in the Bill of Rights that have been incorporated against the states. Douglas then asserts at type of federal "police power" that legitimates intervention to prohibit a state regulations that "sweep unnecessarily broadly and thereby invade the area of protected freedom."[101]

The context of activist national government might also help to explain the gradual incorporation of most of the Bill of Rights into the Fourteenth Amendment's limitations on states, beginning during the early stages of development of the active state[102] and especially in the post-New Deal

---

[100]Mark G. Yudof, *When Government Speaks: Politics, Law, and Government Expression in America*, (Berkeley: University of California Press, 1983), p. 14.

[101]*Griswold v. Connecticut*, 381 U.S. 479, 485 (1965).

[102]Fifth Amendment "eminent domain" in *Chicago, Burlington & Quincy R.R. v. Chicago*, 166 U.S. 226 (1897).

development of the active state[102] and especially in the post-New Deal era.[103]   That is, as the country became more integrated and the governmental power more pervasive generally, it logically could have become increasingly imperative to guarantee fundamental rights of liberty through the national government and not just against the national government.   Akhil Reed Amar notes that the foundation for this increased protection of individuals against the national government, rather than just the protection of the states or people collectively against the national government, was laid in the ratification of the Fourteenth Amendment in 1868.[104]

CONCLUSIONS

Even more than the post 1850s adjustments, the series of constitutional changes which followed the 1930s realignment fundamentally reallocate the balance of power between the national and state governments from that which was set out in the original constitutional order.

---

[102]Fifth Amendment "eminent domain" in *Chicago, Burlington & Quincy R.R. v. Chicago*, 166 U.S. 226 (1897).

[103]*E.g.*, Fourth Amendment "freedom from warrantless search and seizure", in *Mapp v. Ohio*, 367 U.S. 643 (1961).

[104]Akhil Reed Amar, "The Bill of Rights and the Fourteenth Amendment," *Yale Law Journal* 101:1193 (1992).

7. THE 1990S, A BUDGET BATTLE AND A PRESIDENTIAL IMPEACHMENT

One lesson of this research is that the constitutional implications of partisan realignments take time to become fully realized. Looking back at the last few years, this is particularly evident. The Republican victories in the mid-1990s may well have substantial implications for the pre-existing constitutional order, but it may be a few years yet before he extent to which the party's policy agenda is realized may be assessed. One would expect the outcome of 2000 presidential election to be a particularly important factor. In these final pages, the signs of a prospective realignment over the past few years will be delineated, but, given the contingencies remaining, the discussion should be preceded by historical context, which allows an opportunity to review the constitutional theory developed thus far.

The 1800 Realignment

Can the extra-Article V changes to the American constitutional order which followed Jefferson's election to the Presidency in 1800 be squared with the abstracted criteria for legitimate constitutional change? That 1800 was a realignment demonstrates, *ipso facto*, that extraordinary electoral participation swept Jefferson and those of his persuasion into office and the Federalists out of office. Several constitutionally transformative issues also animated the realignment. Specifically, the Jeffersonian's challenged (1) the authority of the federal government, assumed by the Federalists, to implement a commercial political economic system, (2) the aristocratic nature of the American republic under the Federalists, (3) the practice of making criticism of the government a criminal offense, (4) the ethic against political parties in the United States, and (5) expansive federal judicial power, especially the idea of federal common law authority. The partisan equilibrium following the realigning era favored the Jeffersonians, which allowed them to succeed in retrenching federal government authority generally, in retrenching Hamilton's commercialism program but for the national bank and the occasional use of protective tariffs, sustain a party system, eliminate the practice of criminalizing speech critical of the federal government, and reduce the scope of federal judicial authority.

The 1828-32 Realignment

May the informal constitutional transformations following Andrew Jackson's rise to the Presidency be squared, at least in the abstract, with the formal requirements for constitutional amendment? That this was a realigning era indicates, *ipso facto*, that extraordinary electoral participation occurred. Several constitutionally transformative proposals also were constitutive of the realignment. Specifically, Jackson sought (1) to reverse a growing trend toward expanding federal political economy authority, (2) to make the party system more plebiscitary, i.e., more of an institution linking the electorate to government and public policy, and (3) to expand the legislative authority of the President by exempting the office from any deference to the Supreme Court and allowing the veto on grounds other than perceived unconstitutionality. The partisan equilibrium that emerged after the realignment consisted of a new two-party system, with the Whigs now a party and the Democratic-Republicans now simply the Democrats. It stabilized with a less nationally-based political economy and the national bank ultimately destroyed, some federal protection of state interests pursuant to federal commerce clause power, and new democratic complexity to the party system, and some expansion of executive authority, especially the authority to veto legislation on grounds other than constitutionality.

The 1850s Realignment

May the legally deficient post-Civil War Amendments and other Article V-problematic developments in constitutional law following the 1850s be reconciled with the general requirements of Article V? By definition, the realignment indicates extraordinary electoral participation occurred at this time. Several constitutionally transformative issues were involved. Specifically, the new Republican Party, from the 1850s into the 1860s (1) asserted federal authority to restrict slavery in the states, (2) maintained secession from the Union is not permissible, (3) endorsed unilateral military power by the president, (4) encouraged the development of administrative capacities in the national government, and (5) sought to achieve political and social equality for African American males and advancements for African Americans across both genders. The realignment erupted into Civil War, and a viable two-party system did not re-emerge nationally until the 1870s. But as an equilibrium did emerge, it sustained the following: (1) federal authority to restrict slavery, (2) the illegitimacy of secession, (3) that the President may respond to a domestic rebellion with unilateral use of the military, (4) the repudiation of the Jeffersonian/Jacksonian constraints on the administrative capacities of the national government, and (5) the political equality of African American men, best evidenced by the Thirteenth Amendment, the Fifteenth Amendment, and the legislative history version of the Fourteenth Amendment.

The 1890s Realignment

Was the 1890s realignment simply a failed exercise to transform the American constitutional order? The realignment indicates, by definition, that the American electorate was exceptionally involved in the issues of the 1890s. Specifically, in terms of constitutionally transformative issues, the agrarian-led Democratic Party was challenging the industrial and administrative commitments of the Republicans and the pro-industry Democrats rooted in the Civil War-era political developments. The Democrats sought the coinage of silver for the purpose of easing the debt burden of farmers and a restoration of protective tariffs. But the Democrats lost in 1894-96, and the resulting equilibrium left the Republicans holding a greater balance of power over the Democrats, which provided the Republicans an opportunity to consolidate the constitutional status quo ante. In the following years, federal authority to integrate the national market becomes more certain.

The 1930s Realignment

May the Article V-deficient constitutional transformations following the 1930s realignment be reconciled with the general requirements of Article V? Again, by definition, the realignment of the 1930s is evidence of extraordinary electoral participation. In terms of constitutionally transformative proposals, the Democratic Party aimed to (1) legitimize federal government management of some market outcomes, (2) to allow executive-driven federal intervention into state and local economic activity related to, but not the same as, interstate commerce, and (3) eventually to push for the interchangeability between executive agreements and treaties. As an equilibrium emerged in the 1940s, it favored the Democrats and sustains federal management of some market outcomes, unprecedented federal intervention into economic activities traditionally considered solely within state or local purview, and interchangeability between executive agreements and treaties. The administrative republic which emerged from this realigning era has endured, not without its challenges, through the administration of Democrat Bill Clinton.

1994-99 as a Realigning Era

Armed with their Contract with America, the Republicans scored enormous electoral victories in the 1994 elections, just two years after Bill Clinton was elected to the White House so as to make both the executive and legislative branches of the federal government dominated by the Democratic Party. Since the Republican inroads, we have witnessed an extraordinarily long budget battle between the President and Congress, specifically in the winter of 1995, and, more recently, the extraordinary House impeachment and Senate trial of a President. Have we been witnessing an attempt to re-order fundamental American political institutions and practices? The constitutional history pursued in this book suggests a challenge to the constitutional equilibrium following the 1930s realignment is in place, even if it is unclear how this struggle will play out.

Since the New Deal, the Democrats usually have had control of Congress, and, consistent with their Progressive heritage, have typically sought to use the machinery of federal government to address and resolve conflicts and problems. The standard Republican criticism of the Democratic Party in the post-New Deal era has been that the Democratic pro-State philosophy is less efficient than a free-market philosophy and results in a governmental matrix too easily targeted by and too responsive to special interest group. Until the Reagan administration,[1] though, no serious challenge to the New Deal state had been mounted, and Reagan's plan for a New Federalism, which would have returned much administrative power to the states and local governments, fell flat as state and local officials recognized they would inherit the burden of financing established levels of services.[2]

Beginning in 1992, however, conditions marking a prospective realignment of constitutional significance have taken shape. First, there have been signs of a fracturing of consensus about the contemporary constitutional order. The end of the Cold War allowed perhaps unusual attention in the 1992 presidential election to domestic matters. Arguably, priorities changed. "It's the economy, stupid," did become the successful campaign motto of the Clinton campaign. An electoral expectation of new priorities or perhaps new techniques for handling established ones also seems evidenced in the popular support in the 1992 presidential election for the independent candidate H. Ross Perot, who marketed himself as an "outsider" in relation to Washington politics.

Second, the 1994 elections were highly ideological in nature. Upon assuming office in 1993, President Bill Clinton pursued policy initiatives that would be categorized by him and Republican critics as archetypical New Deal liberalism, particularly the health care plan. Clinton likened prospective universal health care to Social Security, which was passed in Roosevelt's New Deal era and is now quite popular. For Republicans, the plan illustrated their claim that the Democratic Party planned only more

---

[1]For an inquiry into whether the election of Ronald Reagan marked the beginning of a realignment in the 1980s, *see* Benjamin Ginsberg and Martin Shefter, "A Critical Realignment? The New Politics, The Reconstituted Right, and the 1984 Election," in Michael Nelson ed., *The Elections of 1984*, (Washington: Congressional Quarterly, Press, 1985) pp. 1-25. For a discussion of the impact the appointment Robert Bork to the U.S. Supreme Court might have had, *see* Bruce A. Ackerman, "Transformative Appointments," 101 *Harvard Law Review* 1164 (1988).

[2]Jeffrey R. Henig, *Public Policy and Federalism: Issues in State and Local Politics*, (New York: St. Martin's Press, 1985), p. 20.

of same brand of New Deal liberalism that, from their perspective, had run amok and damaged the country. The Clinton health care plan failed, and for the November 1994 mid-term congressional elections, the Republican Party made an extraordinary effort to unify the party ideologically against the Democrats, and to make these elections, and even state and local elections also occurring then, a referendum on Democrats generally through a published "Contract with America"[3], signed in September of 1994 by 367 Republican candidates, including 300 Republican candidates for the House of Representatives. The Contract lists a variety of policy objectives, including a balanced budget amendment, welfare reform, tax cuts for families, legal reforms, and congressional term limits. The results of the November 1994 elections were stunning. Republicans gained control of both houses of Congress, a sitting Speaker of the House was defeated, and not a single Republican incumbent Representative, Senator, or governor was defeated. Republicans also regained a majority of state governorships.

Third, the direction of some social policy of the last half-century recently has been reversed. As a result of the elections, a Republican Congress, with the Contract with America in hand, effectively assumed the initiative in public policy making, a role which seems contemplated for the legislative branch under the theory of the original Constitution but which the Presidency usurped during the 1930s, with the Theodore Roosevelt and Woodrow Wilson presidencies as precursors. One of the first provisions of the Contract with America, the Balanced Budget Amendment, narrowly failed the proposal stage in Congress. But the Republican Congress succeeded in passing some welfare reform, which involves tightened eligibility restrictions and the allocation of monies by Congress for distribution to the states in the form of block grants.

Fourth, we have witnessed unusually severe inter-branch conflict in the form an extraordinarily long budget battle and an impeachment of the President. In February of 1995, the President submitted his budget

---

[3]And published as a book: Newt Gingrich et al., *Contract With America: The Bold Plan by Rep. Newt Gingrich, Rep. Dick Armey, and the House Republicans to Change the Nation*, (New York: Times Books, 1994).

proposals to Congress; but Congress' own budget proposal became part of public discourse in the fall of 1995, and upon review of Congress's projections, the President admonished congressional leaders that he would veto elements of the budget plan and the whole package if particular spending cuts were not made less severe. With sufficient Democratic strength in Congress to prevent a congressional override, a presidential veto in November led to the conflict with Congress that resulted in a partial shutdown of the federal government. Comments by the President during this shutdown are particularly revealing. In the early stages of the budget battle, the President cited cuts in Medicare as his primary source of concern about the budget. But, if we recognize that, from an economic perspective, a budget represents a plan of legitimate expenditures in relation to available revenues, its relevance to ideological differences over the scope and place of government is tremendous, and the President's comments on November 15, 1995, would appear to be more revealing as to the conflict between himself and the Republican Congress. In a television interview during the partial government shutdown, the President first reminded listeners of his constitutional authority to veto a budget package that he believes is not in the national interest. He then asserted that the budget plan indicates that the Republicans want to strip the federal government down to national defense and a few other basic services--the classical liberalism model of government of, say, Adam Smith or John Locke, it would seem. And he announced that he was not elected to preside over this type of government, and that if the American people really want this budget, they are entitled to another president. A stopgap measure was approved shortly thereafter, but another impasse emerged, resulting in another partial government shutdown, this one lasting a record three weeks before resolution.

In retrospect, Bill Clinton's decision to allow the federal government to shut down, even if only partially, rather than compromise with Congress seems quite politically adept because it focused public attention precisely on what seems to have been under attack by the Republicans: the administrative capacity of the national government. When monies for community projects are stalled, when people cannot get passports or go to the national parks, and when particular regulatory agencies are shut down or reduced in the number of staff, and when people wonder whether their Social Security or Medicare claims will be processed or checks will arrive, people are quickly reminded of what the national government has done for them lately. Clinton's move also seemed to be successful in terms of public opinion, and it may be significant, in terms of public opinion, that the Contract with America dropped out the discourse of the major candidates for the Republican presidential nomination in 1996. One of the Contract's chief exponents, Senator Phil Gramm, was forced out of the race. Another, Senator Bob Dole, found his campaign weakened, ironically, to the more conservative "populist" candidate Pat Buchanan, who was critical of much of the Republican economic agenda. Dole, in fact, during his campaign once mentioned his belief in an "economic bill of rights" for Americans, a measure which smacks of classic New Deal liberalism. Bill Clinton won the Presidency again in 1996, with claims of steady economic growth, the protection of the environment, and the fostering of a first-rate educational system as the bases for his campaign mantra.

But Clinton's sexual indiscretions with a White House intern led to an expansion of Independent Counsel Kenneth Starr's investigation of Clinton, resulting in a report to Congress alleging eleven impeachable wrongdoings by the President in relation to these indiscretions. Ultimately, the House of Representatives voted to impeach the President on two articles of impeachment, and the Senate tried the case, although it acquitted the President. That the impeachment fits within partisan-struggle scenario rather than strict rule of law is not exceedingly difficult to establish. Public opinion generally favored the President throughout the investigation and the impeachment process. House Republicans pressed onward with the investigation despite the polls, and, in 1998, for first the first time in decades, a president's party gained seats during a mid-term election. Despite these election returns, the House Judiciary Committee, on strict party lines, voted to approve four articles of impeachment; and largely by partisan vote, the House voted to impeach the President on two counts. When the Senate voted to acquit the President, all Democrats voted to acquit on both charges, and a few Republicans joined them. A majority still voted to convict the President, but a two-thirds majority is needed to convict, and the Democrats had sufficient numbers to preclude such a majority. Public opinion generally disapproved of the Republican handling of the impeachment process, and the President enjoyed high job-approval ratings throughout the process.

Fourth, the issue area that has seemed at the core of these potentially transformative politics is the same issue area that has been at the core of every realigning period in American politics: the scope of federal government economic power in relation to the power of the states. The Balanced Budget Amendment would have kept spending down and constrained the size of the federal government. The Republican initiative of making welfare a prerogative of the states through block grants now seems rooted in James Monroe's approach to federalism in the late 1810s and early 1820s. The United States Supreme Court's April 1995 ruling in *United States v. Lopez*[4], seems perfectly consistent with the Republican agenda in 1994, i.e., either to limit the growth of federal government economic power in relation to state government, or simply reverse it. The case involved the constitutionality of Gun-Free School Zones Act of 1990, which forbid any person to possess a gun in any area he or she knew to be school zone. The Act was premised on the interstate commerce authority of the federal government, the same authority that now underpins the modern federal bureaucratic structures, collective bargaining, Social Security, etc., following expansive readings of the clause in the 1930s. Writing for the Court, Chief Justice William Rehnquist held that in no sense is the possession of a gun in a school zone an economic activity.[5] Justice Rehnquist notes that the federal government did not present any formal findings of fact regarding the burdens on interstate commerce that it aims to reach, but also acknowledges that the government is not required to present such findings of fact. Yet Rehnquist obfuscates the tradition set forth in *Carolene Products* that even in the absence of supporting facts, federal legislation affecting commerce "is not to be pronounced unconstitutional unless in the light of the facts made known or generally assumed it is such a character as to preclude the assumption that it rests upon some rational basis. . . ."[6]

This decision represents a rare instance in post-New Deal America in

---

[4] 63 LW 4343 (1995).

[5] 63 LW at 4346-47.

[6] *United States v. Carolene Products Co.*, 304 U.S. 144, 152 (1938).

which the Supreme Court has said that Congress had no basis for its decision that some matter affects interstate commerce and invalidated the legislation. That this case involved schools also seems important, because education traditionally has been under the purview of state authority but recently a possible object of a greater federal involvement, in light of the asserted link between educational attainment and the economic success of this country. *Lopez* therefore could stand as precedent against attempts by Congress or the Executive Office to expand federal government involvement in education in relation to the states, or as a stepping stone for those who wish to challenge federal commerce authority as it stands now in other contexts. Indeed, Rehnquist's opinion suggests he is positioning the decision to serve this purpose:

> . . . [I]f Congress can, pursuant to its Commerce Clause power, regulative activities that adversely affect the learning environment, then, *a fortiori*, it also can regulate the educational process directly. Congress could determine that a school's curriculum has a "significant" effect on the extent of classroom learning. As a result, Congress could mandate a federal curriculum for local elementary and secondary schools because what is taught in local schools has a significant "effect on classroom learning," . . ., and that, in turn, has a substantial effect on interstate commerce.[7]

The federal courts also have weakened national protection of affirmative action, a policy which Democrats traditionally have favored. Since at least *Brown v. Board of Education*,[8] race had been considered a "suspect classification" under Equal Protection doctrine, requiring courts to examine legislation or official actions that make use of race with "strict scrutiny," *i.e.*, for whether this use is a necessary means to a compelling state interest. In *Bakke v. Regents of the University of California*,[9] the

---

[7]63 LW at 4348.

[8]347 U.S. 483 (1954).

[9]438 U.S. 265 (1978).

California,[9] the Supreme Court, in a polarized and non-majoritarian decision, applied strict scrutiny to the race-conscious admissions program at the University of California at Davis Medical School but still upheld the principle of affirmative action under the Equal Protection Clause, provided that race-consciousness is used to vindicate constitutional entitlement. The Court also found special latitude for educational administrators to consider race in admissions decisions to universities under the First Amendment, for the purpose of achieving diversity in student bodies. But since 1978, the Court gradually has narrowed the grounds for the legitimacy of affirmative action, typically requiring more of a showing that the beneficiaries of affirmative action are merely being compensated for demonstrable harm done to them because of their race.[10] The Supreme Court had held federal affirmative action programs to a lower standard of scrutiny than that required for state governmental uses of "suspect classifications,"[11] but last year held that federal affirmative action programs also should be required to show that the use of race is a necessary means a to a compelling state interest.[12] More recently, the Fifth Circuit held that the race-conscious affirmative action program used in the admissions process at The University of Texas School of Law is unconstitutional and declared the "diversity" justification illegitimate.[13] The Supreme Court denied writ of certiorari.

In recent years, moreover, the Supreme Court has carved out a greater scope of state immunity from federal law. At the close of the 1998-99 term, the Supreme Court issued three decisions by which it made states

---

[9]438 U.S. 265 (1978).

[10]*See, e.g., City of Richmond v. J.A. Croson Co.*, 488 U.S. 469 (1989).

[11]*See Metro Broadcasting, Inc. v. Federal Communications Commission*, 497 U.S. 547 (1990).

[12]*Adarand Constructors, Inc v. Pena*, 115 S.Ct. 2097 (1995).

[13]*Hopwood v. Texas*, 78 F.3d 932 (5th Cir. 1996).

immune from state employees for violations of federal labor law,[14] from patent owners for infringement of their patents by state universities and agencies,[15] and from persons bringing unfair competition suits over states' activities in the marketplace.[16] A *New York Times* article on these cases describes the Court in a manner wholly consistent with the partisan politics described in this book, *i.e.*, as an institution animating American constitutional development from the vantage point of its partisan heritage and leanings:

> It was clear this from the courtroom scene this morning and from the 185 pages of often impassioned prose the Court produced in the three cases that, for these Justices, the question of the proper allocation of authority within the American system is not abstract or theoretical but urgent and fundamental, with the two sides holding irreconcilable visions of what the Constitution's framers had in mind.[17]

---

[14]*Alden v. Maine*, No. 98-436 (U.S. Sup. Ct., June 23, 1999).

[15]*Florida Prepaid Postsecondary Ed. Expense Bd. v. College Savings Bank*, No. 98-531 (U.S. Sup. Ct., June 23, 1999).

[16]*College Savings Bank v. Florida Prepaid Postsecondary Ed. Expense Bd.*, No. 98-149 (U.S. Sup. Ct., June 23, 1999).

[17]Linda Greenhouse, "States Are Given New Legal Shield by Supreme Court, In Shift of Power from Congress, Justices Bar Some Lawsuits," *The New York Times*, National, Thursday, June 24, 1999.

BIBLIOGRAPHY

Bruce A. Ackerman, *We the People: Transformations*, (Cambridge: Harvard University Press, 199-).

_____, *We the People: Foundations*, (Cambridge: Harvard University Press, 1991).

_____, "Constitutional Politics/Constitutional Law," 99 *Yale Law Journal* 453(1989).

_____, "Transformative Appointments," 101 *Harvard Law Review* 1164 (1988).

_____, "The Storrs Lectures: Discovering the Constitution," 93 *Yale Law Journal* 1013 (1984).

_____ and David Golove, "Is NAFTA Constitutional?", 108 *Harvard Law Review* 799 (1995).

Adamany, David, "Legitimacy, Realigning Elections, and the Supreme Court," 1973 *Wisconsin Law Review* 790 (1973).

Agresto, John, *The Supreme Court and Constitutional Democracy*, (Ithaca: Cornell University Press, 1985).

Amar, Akhil Reed, "The Consent of the Governed," 94 *Columbia Law Review* 457 (1994).

_____, "The Bill of Rights and the Fourteenth Amendment," 101 *Yale Law Journal* 1193 (1992).

_____, "Philadelphia Revisited: Amending the Constitution

Outside Article V," 55 *The University of Chicago Law Review* 1043 (1988).

Arkes, Hadley, *Beyond the Constitution*, (Princeton: Princeton University Press, 1990).

Bailyn, Bernard et al., *The Great Republic: A History of the American People*, 2nd ed., Vol. 1 (Lexington: D.C. Heath & Co., 1981).

Banning, Lance, *The Jeffersonian Persuasion*, (Ithaca: Cornell University Press, 1978).

Berger, Raoul, *Government By Judiciary: The Transformation of the Fourteenth Amendment*, (Cambridge: Harvard University Press, 1977).

Berns, Walter, *Taking the Constitution Seriously*, (New York: Simon & Schuster, 1987).

Bessette, Joseph M., and Jeffrey Tulis, eds., *The Presidency in the Constitutional Order*, (Baton Rouge: Louisiana State University Press, 1981).

Blau, Joseph L., ed., *Social Theories of Jacksonian Democracy: Representative Writings of the Period 1825-1850*, (New York: The Liberal Arts Press, 1954).

Bobbitt, Philip C., *Constitutional Intepretation*, (Oxford: Blackwell, 1991).

Bork, Robert H., *The Tempting of America: The Political Seduction of the Law* (New York: Simon & Schuster, 1990).

Buel, Richard, Jr., *Securing the Revolution*, (Ithaca: Cornell University Press, 1972).

Brady, David W., *Critical Elections and Congressional Policy Making*, (Stanford: Stanford University Press, 1988).

Brest, Paul and Sanford Levinson, *Processes of Constitutional Decisionmaking: Cases and Materials*, 2nd ed., (Boston: Little Brown &

Co., 1983).

Burnham, Walter Dean, *Critical Elections and the Mainsprings of American Politics* (New York: W.W. Norton, 1970).

_____, "Critical Realignment: Dead or Alive?" in Byron E. Shafer, ed., *The End of Realignment? Interpreting American Electoral Eras*, (Madison: The University of Wisconsin Press, 1992).

_____, "The 1896 System: An Analysis," in Paul Kleppner, et al., *The Evolution of American Electoral Systems*, (Westport: Greenwood Press, 1981).

Campbell, James E., "Sources of the New Deal Realignment: The Contributions of Conversion and Mobilization to Partisan Change," 38 *Western Political Quarterly* (September 1985) 357-76.

Casper, Jonathan D., "The Supreme Court and National Policy Making," 70 *American Political Science Review* 50 (1976).

Ceaser, James W., *Presidential Selection: Theory and Development*, (Princeton: Princeton University Press, 1979).

Chambers, William Nisbet, *Political Parties in a New Nation*, (New York: Oxford University Press, 1963).

_____, and Walter Dean Burnham, *The American Party Systems: Stages of Political Development*, 2nd ed., (New York: Oxford University Press, 1975).

Charles, Joseph, *The Origins of the American Party System*, (Institute of Early American History and Culture, 1956).

Clubb, Jerome M., William H. Flanagan, and Nancy H. Zingdale, *Partisan Realignment: Voters, Parties, and Government in American History*, (Beverly Hills: Sage, 1980).

Corwin, Edward S., "The Constitution as Instrument and as Symbol," 30 *American Political Science Review* 1071 (1936).

Cunningham, Noble E., Jr., The Jeffersonian Republicans: The Formation of a Party Organization, (Chapel Hill: University of North Carolina, 1957).

Currie, David P., *The Constitution in the Supreme Court: The First Hundred Years, 1789-1888*, (Chicago: The University of Chicago Press, 1985).

_____, *The Constitution in the Supreme Court: The Second Century, 1888-1986*, (Chicago: The University of Chicago Press, 1990).

Dahl, Robert A., "Decision-Making in a Democracy: The Supreme Court as a National Policy-Maker," 6 *Journal of Public Law* 179 (1957).

Dodd, "Social Legislation and the Courts," 28 *Political Science Quarterly* 1 (1913).

Dudziak, Mary, "Desegregation as a Cold War Imperative," 41 *Stanford Law Review* 61 (1988).

Dworkin, Ronald, *Law's Empire*, (Cambridge: Harvard University Press, 1986).

Ellis, Richard E., "The Persistence of Antifederalism after 1789," in R. Beeman et al. eds., *Beyond Confederation*, (Chapel Hill: University of North   Carolina Press, 1987).

Finn, John, *Constitutions in Crisis: Political Violence and the Rule of Law*, (New York: Oxford University Press, 1991).

Fisher, Louis, *Constitutional Dialogues: Constitutional Interpretation as Political Process* (Washington, D.C: CQ Press)

Fishkin, James S., *The Voice of the People: Public Opinion and Democracy*, (New Haven: Yale University Press, 1995).

_____, *Democracy and Deliberation: New Directions for Democratic Reform*, (New Haven: Yale University Press, 1991).

Foner, Eric, *Reconstruction: America's Unfinished Revolution, 1863-*

1877, (New York: Harper & Row, 1988).

Frisch, Morton J., and Richard G. Stevens, eds., *The Political Thought of American Statesmen*, (Itasca: F.E. Peacock, 1973).

Funston, Richard, "The Supreme Court and Critical Elections," 69 *American Political Science Review* 795 (1975).

Gates, John, "The American Supreme Court and Electoral Realignment: A Critical Review," 8 *Social Science History* 267 (1984).

Gingrich, Newt, et al., *Contract With America: The Bold Plan by Rep. Newt Gingrich, Rep. Dick Armey, and the House Republicans to Change the Nation*, (New York: Times Books, 1994).

Ginsberg, Benjamin, "Elections and Public Policy," 70 *American Political Science Review* 41 (1976).

_____, and Martin Shefter, "A Critical Realignment? The New Politics, The Reconstituted Rights, and the 1984 Election," in Michael Nelson ed., *The Elections of 1984*, (Washington: CQ Press, 1985), pp. 1-25.

Goodwyn, Lawrence, *The Populist Moment: A Short History of the Agrarian Revolt in America*, (Oxford: Oxford University Press, 1978).

Greenhouse, Linda, "States Are Given New Legal Shield by Supreme Court, In Shift of Power from Congress, Justices Bar Some Lawsuits," *The New York Times*, National, Thursday, June 24, 1999

Hammond, Banks, *Banks and Politics in America from the Revolution to the Civil War*, (Princeton: Princeton University Press, 1957).

Hanson, Russell L., *The Democratic Imagination in America: Conversations With Our Past*, (Princeton: Princeton University Press, 1979).

Harris, William F., *The Interpretable Constitution*, (Baltimore: Johns Hopkins University Press, 1993)

Henig, Jeffrey R., *Public Policy and Federalism: Issues in State and Local Politics*, (New York: St. Martin's Press, 1985).

Hofstadter, Richard, *The Idea of a Party System: The Rise of Legitimate Opposition in the United States, 1780-1840*, (Berkeley : University of California Press, 1969).

Holt, Martin F., *The Political Crisis of the 1850s*, (New York, 1978)

Jacobsohn, Gary, *The Supreme Court and the Decline of Constitutional Aspiration*, (Totowa: Rowman & Littlefield, 1986).

John J. Janssen, "Dualist Constitutional Theory and The Republican Revolution of 1800," 12 *Constitutional Commentary* 381 (1995).

Jefferson, Thomas, *Notes on the State of Virginia*, (W. Peden, ed., New York: W.W. Norton, 1954).

Kelly, Alfred, Winfred A. Harbison, and Herman Belz, *The American Constitution: Its Origins and Development*, 6th ed., (New York: W.W. Norton, 1983).

Key, V.O., "A Theory of Critical Elections," 17 *Journal of Politics* 3 (1955).

Kincaid, John, "State Court Protections of Individual Rights Under State Constitutions: The New Judicial Federalism," 61 *Journal of State Government* 163 (1988).

Klarman, Michael J., "Constitutional Fact/Constitutional Fiction: A Critique of Bruce Ackerman's Theory of Constitutional Moments," 44 *Stanford Law Review* 759 (1992).

Kluger, Richard, *Simple Justice*, (New York: Vintage, 1975).

Ladd, Everett Carl, "Like Waiting for Godot: The Uselessness of 'Realignment' for Understanding Change in Contemporary American Politics," in Byron E. Shafer, ed, *The End of Realignment? Interpreting American Electoral Eras*, (Madison: The University of Wisconsin Press, 1991).

Levinson, Sanford, ed., *Responding to Imperfection: The Theory and Practice of Constitutional Amendment*, (Princeton: Princeton University Press, 1995).

Levinson, Sanford, "Accounting for Constitutional Change (Or, How Many Times Has the Unied States Constitution Been Amended? (a) <26; (b) 26; (c)   >26; (D) All of the Above)," 8 *Constitutional Commentary* 409 (1991).

Locke, John, *The Second Treatise on Civil Government*, (New York: Prometheus Books, 1986).

Lowi, Theodore J., *The End of Liberalism: The Second Republic of the United States*, 2nd ed., (New York: Norton, 1979).

Madison, James, Alexander Hamilton, and John Jay, *The Federalist Papers*, No. 41 (Clinton Rossiter, ed.) (New York: New American library, 1961).

Manchester, William, *The Glory and the Dream: A Narrative History of America, 1932-1972*, (Toronto: Bantam, 1975).

Mansfield, Harvey C., *America's Constitutional Soul*, (Baltimore: Johns Hopkins University Press, 1991).

Marshall, J., Address on Constitutionality of Alien and Sedition Laws, in Frisch and R. Stevens, eds., The Political Thought of American Statesmen, (Itasca: F.E. Peacock, 1973).

Massey, Calvin R., "State Sovereignty and the Tenth and Eleventh Amendments," 56 *University of Chicago Law Review*, 113 (1989).

McCloskey, Robert G., *The American Supreme Court*, 2nd ed. (Chicago: The University of Chicago Press, 1992).

McCormick, Richard P., "Political Development and the Second Party System," in William Nisbet Chambers and Walter Dean Burnham, eds., The American Party Systems: Stage of Political Development, (New York: Oxford University Press, 1975).

McCormick, Richard, *The Party Period and Public Policy: American Politics from the Age of Jackson to the Progressive Era*, (New York: Oxford University Press, 1986).

McKitrick, Eric L., *Andrew Johnson and Reconstruction*, (New York: Oxford University Press, 1960).

Meyers, Marvin, *The Jacksonian Persuasion: Politics & Belief*, (Stanford: Stanford University Press, 1960).

Milkis, Sidney M., *The President and the Parties: The Transformation of the American Party System Since the New Deal*, (New York: Oxford University Press, 1993).

Morison, Samuel Eliot, *The Oxford History of the American People: Volume Three, 1869-1963*, (New York: Penguin, 1972).

O'Fallon, James, "Marbury," 44 *Stanford Law Review* 219 (1992).

Pound, Roscoe, "Liberty of Contract," 18 *Yale Law Journal* 454 (1909).

Randall, J. G., *Constitutional Problems Under Lincoln*, rev. ed., (Glouster, Mass.: Peter Smith, 1963).

Rawle, W., *A View of the Constitution of the United States of America*, 2nd ed., (1825).

Richardson, James D., ed., *A Compilation of the Messages and Papers of the Presidents, 1789-1897*, 10 vols., (Washington: U.S. Government Printing Office, 1896-1899).

Rowe, Gary D., "The Sound of Silence: *United States v. Hudson & Goodwin*, Jeffersonian Ascendancy, and the Abolition of Federal Common Law Crimes, 101 *Yale Law Journal* 919 (1992).

Schafer, Byron E., "The Notion of an Electoral Order: The Structure of Electoral Politics at the Accession of George Bush," in Byron E. Shafer, ed., *The End of Realignment? Interpreting American Electoral Eras*, (Madison, The University of Wisconsin Press, 1991).

Schlesinger, Arthur M., Jr., *The Age of Jackson*, (Boston: Little, Brown & Company, 1950).

Schouler, James, *History of the United States of America Under the Constitution, Vol. II*, rev. ed., (Dodd, Mead, & Co., 1970), p. 27.

Sherry, Suzanna, "The Ghost of Liberalism Past," 105 *Harvard Law Review* 918 (1992).

Silbey, Joel H., "Beyond Realignment and Realignment Theory: American Political Eras, 1789-1989," in Byron E. Shafer, ed., *The End of Realignment? Interpreting American Electoral Eras*, (Madison, The University of Wisconsin, 1991).

Sisson, Daniel, *The American Revolution of 1800*, (New York: Alfred A. Knopf, 1974).

Skowronek, Stephen, *Building a New Amrican State: The Expansion of National Administrative Capacities, 1877-1920*, (Cambridge: Cambridge University Press, 1982).

Skowronek, Stephen, *The Politics Presidents Make: Leadership from John Adams to George Bush* (Cambridge: Harvard University Press, 1993)

Stampp, Kenneth M., The Era of Reconstruction, 1865-1877, (New York: Alfred A. Knopf, 1982).

Storing, Herbert J., *What the Anti-Federalists Were For*, vol. 1. of Storing's *The Complete Anti-Federalist*, (Chicago: University of Chicago Press, 1981).

Sundquist. James L., *Dynamics of the Party System: Alignment and Realignment of Political Parties in the United States*, rev. ed, (Washington: Brookings Institution, 1983).

Sunstein, Cass, *The Partial Constitution*, (Cambridge: Harvard University Press, 1993)

Tindall, George Brown, *America, A Narrative History, Vol. I*, (New York:

W.W. Norton, 1984).

Tulis, Jeffrey K., *The Rhetorical Presidency*, (Princeton: Princeton University Press, 1987).

Tushnet, Mark, *Red, White and Blue: A Critical Analysis of Constitutional Law*, (Cambridge: Harvard University Press, 1988).

Unger, Roberto Mangaberia, *The Critical Legal Studies Movement* (Cambridge: Harvard University Press, 1988).

U.S. Bureau of the Census, *Historical Statistics in the United States: Colonial Times to 1957*, (Washington, D.C., 1960).

Wattenberg, Martin P., *The Decline of American Political Parties, 1952-1984*, (Cambridge: Harvard University Press, 1986).

Wechsler, Herbert, "Toward Neutral Principles of Constitutional Law," 73 *Harvard Law Review* 1 (1959).

White, Leonard D., *The Jeffersonians*, (New York: MacMillan, 1951).

Wiebe, Robert H., *The Search for Order, 1877-1920*, (New York: Hill and Wang, 1967).

Wills, Gary, *Lincoln at Gettysburg: The Words That Remade America*, (New York: Simon & Schuster, 1992), p. 132.

Young, James Sterling, *The Washington Community 1800-1828*, (New York: Harcourt, Brace, Jovanovich, 1966).

Yudof, Mark G., *When Government Speaks: Politics, Law, and Government Expression in America*, (Berkeley: University of California Press, 1983).

TABLE OF CASES

Robbins v. Shelby County, 120 U.S. 489 (1887)
Schecter Poultry Co. v. United States, 295 U.S. 495 (1935)
The Slaughterhouse Cases, 83 U.S. 36 (1872)
Sturges v. Crowinshield, 17 U.S. (4 Wheat.) 122 (1819)
United States v. Carolene Products Co., 304 U.S. 144 (1938)
United States v. Darby, 312 U.S. 100 (1941)
United States v. E.C. Knight Co., 156 U.S. 1 (1895)
United States v. Hudson and Goodwin, 11 U.S. (7 Cranch) 32 (1812)
United States v. Lopez, 63 LW 4343 (1995)
United States v. Worrall, 2 U.S. (2 Dall.) 384 (1798)
Veazie Bank v. Fenno, 74 U.S. (8 Wall.) 533 (1869)
Ware v. Hylton, 3 U.S. (3 Dall.) 199 (1796)
Wabash, St. L. & P. Ry. v. Illinois, 118 U.S. 557 (1886)
Welton v. Missouri, 91 U.S. 275 (1875)
West Coast Hotel Co. v. Parrish, 300 U.S. 379 (1937)
Wickard v. Filburn, 317 U.S. 111 (1942)
Wilson v. Black Bird Creek Marsh, 27 U.S. (2 Pet.) 245 (1829)
Worcester v. Georgia, 31 U.S. (5 pet.) 515 (1832)

ABOUT THE AUTHOR

John J. Janssen is an associate with the law firm of Brin & Brin, P.C., in Edinburg, Texas, where he practices civil litigation in state and federal court. He is the author of articles in *Constitutional Commentary* and *The Review of Litigation*, and has taught political science at various colleges or universities. Janssen holds a J.D. and Ph.D. from The University of Texas at Austin, an M.A. from Yale University, and a B.A. from Southwestern University.